FROM **A POVERTY** MINDSET TO **A WEALTHY** MINDSET

Empowering Women Mentally, Physically and Financially.

LASHIELA HOLMES

From A Poverty Mindset To A Wealthy Mindset

Copyright @ 2018 LaShiela Holmes

All rights reserved. Printed in the United States of America. No part of this book may be used or reproduced in any manner whatsoever without written permission except in the case of brief quotations embodied in critical articles or reviews.

Published by:

Relentless Publishing House, LLC

www.relentlesspublishing.com

Eidited by: FIVERR

ISBN: 9781948829267

First Edition: October 2019

10 9 8 7 6 5 4 3 2 1

Acknowledgements

First, I want to Thank God for equipping me to write this book to help women all over the nation. Giving me the courage to tell my story how he has kept me through my journey. Next, I am thankful for my four children without them I would not be able to tell you my story of being a successful single woman and mother. Raising my children was the greatest blessing in my life that brought both pain and joy. They have taught me how to be a mother, how to love beyond the pain, they taught me that it's ok to fail and still be loved. They taught me what true sacrifice was, they taught me how to be strong in the tough seasons. They taught me how to be the greatest mother and woman that I could be. I have been a single parent for over 23 years, and I raised my children pretty much by myself with the help from a few people God brought into my life. I have done and seen it all as a young woman and mother going through life with all the struggles that come with being a single woman and mother. What I have learnt through my journey is that you can make it as a single woman and mother. Regardless of the obstacles and people that could discourage you or push you to give up, you too can be a successful mother and woman all at the same time.

Introduction

The reason I have written this book is to restore woman back to themselves spiritually, mentally, physically and financially. As women we go through a lot of things with no help when needed. I know what it is to me a single mother with no one to help during those difficult times. I know what it is not being able to call on your family for help, simply because they do not have the resources to help. I know what it is to be broke without money, broken from a relationship, broken from your family and friends. I know what it is to not have the right type of friends in your corner when you just want someone to confide too. I know what it is to have children fathers that does not help or care about the child. I know how it feels to be alone and lonely. I know how it feels that you are the bread and butter for your family. I know how you feel when you're ready to throw in the towel. I know how it feels when you are depressed, angry, frustrated etc. I know what is feels like when you start to get yourself together and everyone gets jealous of you, and usually they are the same people that would not give you a helping hand. I know how it feels to accomplish things and your family are not happy for you. I have seen it, lived it and faced it and God still brought me out smelling like roses and not the smoke that I went through. This book will help you rediscover a new and better you. You can finally leave the past in the past and start a fresh new journey. Help is on the way. Sit back, enjoy the read and let's change you so everything around you can change. It all starts with you. Are you ready to face the truth and get your life back on track?

Contents

ACKNOWLEDGEMENTS 3
INTRODUCTION 4
MY STORY 7
WHAT IS POVERTY 21
CONFIDENCE 23
BROKEN PEOPLE 29
SLAVE MENTALITY 40
I'M TIRED OF MY KIDS 46
RENEW MY MIND 49
DATING WHILE RAISING KIDS 53
WHAT'S MY LOVE LANGUAGES 57
MY FINANCES 58
MY FINANCES 62
HOW TO COMMUNICATE WITH CHILDREN 65
YOUR 18 GET OUT 68
UNCOMFORTABLE SEASON 73
EXERCISE 77
CONCLUSION 79
RESOURCES 80

MY STORY

It all started in a small country town in Texas. I grew up there until I was 19 years old. Growing up in the country was okay. I came from a nuclear family comprising of my Dad, Mom and siblings. My father was a full blooded Native American Cheyenne-Arapaho and my mother was a Black American. We were six children, three boys and three girls. I was the third child and the oldest daughter. I was the only dark-skinned child. My other siblings were light skinned like my Dad. I got teased a lot because of my dark skin, people always questioned me on why and how I was the only dark child and everyone else was lighter than me, literally I was midnight black and they were all yellow like the sun, but I was never able to answer that question. I knew I was different, but it never bothered me until my siblings would make fun of me for being dark. Like with most siblings, you often get teased about something. I was called blackie or darkie when they got mad but that never bothered me either. I guess I was born with tough skin and very high confidence. Being the black sheep of the family to me was a blessing. If for anything, that was my special trait which was my uniqueness. I felt like an outcast in my own family because I was different and did not know why at the time when I was younger but as I got older God revealed to me why I was different from my family.

In every family God will appoint a chosen child and I have to be that chosen one. Did I ask for it? NO but I was called and there was nothing that I could do about it. So, all my life I have been different and have thought different from my family, but still I did not understand why at the time.

Growing up in a large size household where both parents were high school dropouts, we did not have much to look for in the future. Although my dad dropped out and went into the military and was there for 25 years. We did not have to move around like some military families because he was in the army national guard. We may not have had a lot, but we had structured because my dad was a sergeant in the army and so he taught us to be disciplined like soldiers. Growing up as a kid, I didn't consider my family to be poor because we had the necessities for our family. Little did I know that we were considered poor, I guess I can say that my bottom was not bottom like some other kids growing up. I remember those paper food stamps and government cheese as they called it back then. Back then I grew up which some would consider just above the poor line. We were very rich in spirit and were blessed. My parents struggled but they made it work, we were the first black family to move into a white neighborhood. My dad did not look black he was just raised by a black family; he was adopted by my grandparents when he was an infant. So, we got a lot of things because of his skin color. When my dad found us a house on Main street the white neighborhood, the owners of the house had met with him to give him the key and my mom went with him that day. The white owner thought that my mom was his maid, but my dad told him that she was his wife. My parents said, "you should have seen the look on the landlords face". My dad took the key and smiled at the landlord. That story still tickles me to this day about the look on the white landlord's face when he realized that he rented his house to a black family. We stayed in that house for about 12 years until everyone was almost grown up. We also were brought up in church. Our mother made sure we went to church every Sunday and that was because she was the bus driver and had to pick up everyone for church. We attended Greater Faith Mission a C.O.G.I.C Holiness church taught by Pastor Gary Thomas which was our cousin on my grandparents' side. We attended church morning, noon and night, well that's how it felt. I came from a very religious background and I was taught from a young age about God but did not understand it until I was older. Proverbs 22:6 "Train up a child in the way he should go: and when he is old, he will not depart from it." That scripture did come to pass. When I was around 14 years old, I went to live with my grandparents and that's when my life changed for the better. Is was 6 children in the house so we all could not get the attention that we needed as children because both of my parents worked, and they did the best they knew how to do, coming from dysfunctional backgrounds themselves. My grandparents owned their land and house but did not have millions in the bank at the time.

My grandparents both were on fixed incomes, but they made their money stretched, and had some money stored up for rainy days. It may not have been hundreds of thousands, but it was enough in case a rainy day did occur. My grandparents showed me how to be stable, what real love was about and how to own my own things. My grandfather treated me like a queen, there was nothing that I could do wrong in that man's eyes. They really spoiled me even when I was living with my parents. But while living with my grandparents, I received that one on one love and it made me feel like I mattered in life. My grandmother showed me how to be a woman of her own by working and providing for myself and others, she showed me how a mother loves her children, and how a wife is supposed to be with a husband. My grandmother instilled the word of God in me as well. When I became a teenager around 16 years old, I got a job at the Subway and started making money. I knew that I liked to spend money and my grandparents always kept a stash and was never broke so I grasped that and wanted to go get my own money. They taught me to make money and save some money. My grandfather died when I was around 10 or 11.

My parents worked all the time and had 6 kids at the time, so saving was not what they could afford to do. I started working and I did not stop. Two things happened when I turned 16 years old, I started my first job and got pregnant too. Being pregnant at 16 really was not much of a struggle because I had a support system and I knew how to work on a job. I had my son in my junior year, completing high school was not a maybe, it was a must in my family if you graduated high school my parents were proud. I lived in the country where if you missed school, it was like living a boring life because the party was at the school. School was fun because everyone would be at school having fun and if you were at home basically you would have to wait until everyone got out of school to hang out. Before I had my son, my parents separated and the family really fell apart. After I had my son in March 1996 of my Junior year I became very ill around April and had to have a surgery immediately because I had gall stones in my gall bladder that needed to be removed, but at the time that they found them, they had been in my gall bladder for some time that they developed poison in my body that needed to be removed before they could operate on me. That procedure of removing the poison for the gall stones that lasted about a week before they could operate. I begged the doctor to let me go back to school and have the operation the next week, so I would not miss school anymore. I just had my son in March, and all this went down at the end of April, the school arranged for someone to drop off my work while I was out on maternity leave for my son. I kept thinking that I already missed so much work, so I wanted to get back to school. The doctor let me go home on a Friday, so I could return to school on Monday to get things in order and let the school know what was going on with my illness, but I did not make it through the weekend and my mom had to rush me back to the hospital for immediate surgery. So, by the time I got out of the hospital school was over, I did not get to take the tests for 11th grade. So, when school started the next year, I went to the principal and explained what happened at the end of the year that I was in the hospital, so he let me take all the tests that was required so I could be a senior and I graduated with an advanced diploma which means I took more classes than I had too, not too bad for a teenage mother. The last month of school before I graduated, I got myself a car because I continued to work while I was in school and I had a $500 tax refund which was enough to get a car. My son's grandmother on his dad's side took me to get a car. Mrs. Johnnie Ray (RIP) that lady also taught me a lot growing up. She worked in a nursing home and went to school to get some education. She always told me that I was black and so I had to be one step ahead of them. I knew who she referred to as them, so I had to level up at some point and get some type of education. God will always put people in your life when you think that you do not have anyone to teach you on a level that you need in your life. When I graduated from high school, I moved into a 1-bedroom house. I did not have to because I stayed with my grandmother at the time and my grandma did not want me to leave. When I told her that I was moving into my own house she looked at me and said, "when you leave don't come back either", she was upset that I wanted to leave. I wanted to leave so I could do the things I wanted to do like party, so I did just that with my son's father. Then after a year my brother and his family moved in and I continued to work and party. I was making enough money at that time back then; it wasn't difficult for me to make money.

MY STORY

I was taught how to make money, but I knew nothing about investing. However, I knew how to save money from my grandparents because I watched my parents spend the little money we had to provide for the household. They could not really save for a rainy day because of not having enough income coming into the house.

I was doing my thing working and living life as a young adult. I also gave my grandmother money just because, she did not need it but that was a thank you gift for taking care of my son while I worked and enjoyed my life as a young adult. I was the one in the family that made sure everyone was good. I moved into a 1-bedroom house. At about 3 months into the lease, the landlord a white lady that I rented from told me that she could help me get on HUD, I did not know what that meant. I knew about food stamps but not the housing program. My landlord handled everything for me all I had to do was pay $25 rent. After she helped me get on HUD, I went from paying $275 a month to $25 a month. At that time, I did not know what was going on but to be honest, I felt like poverty was still following me from my parents. I got to know about the welfare system from people around. I did not go to college because to be honest getting high school diploma was good enough for my parents, and since college was not talked about alot I didn't think it was necessary for me. I continued to work until I was about 19 and I started talking with a coworker that was older than I and she was talking about a hair school in the next town which was about 1 ½ hours away. I became interested and so I went ahead to find out more about the school because I knew that there was more to my life than living in a country town and working like a slave. I enrolled in Exposito Hair School. The school was very classy and was predominantly white. It was a beautiful school, but they mostly taught about hairstyles for white people and I wanted to learn hairstyles for black people, so it did not work out for me. Don't get me wrong, I had a few black clients, but I needed more experience with making hairstyles for black woman. I ended up not continuing with the school. Later after my 21st birthday I found out I was pregnant again and I moved to Dallas, Texas. That is where my life changed, the city life had so many opportunities there, but I was pregnant with my second child. I went and got a job and started working just few months after I got to Dallas. I was staying with my sister and her family. It was such an uncomfortable situation not because of my sister and her family, but because I was pregnant and due for my second child, yet I had no car, house or money. It was especially uncomfortable because I was coming from a situation where I always had money in my pocket and a car to drive. So, the entire situation did not just sit well with me, 30 days later and I started my job, I got an apartment. Then after I had my daughter I went and bought a car for myself. I decided to give myself sometime off after my pregnancy. Four months later, I got another job that paid me more. Now I had been in Dallas for over a year now, I was just working and taking care of my 2 kids at the time. Two years later my grandma became ill and I had to decide if wanted to take her in my home or let her go to a nursing home until she gets better. I decided to take care of her myself because she took care of me when I was younger. I remember I went to stay with her when I was 14, not because I had issues with my parents but I just prefferred to stay with her and she spoiled me.

I went and picked her up from Amarillo, Tx where she was admitted in the hospital and she came to live with me. Once she got to Dallas, Tx things went downhill for me. I found out that I was pregnant with my third kid and I had to move out of my apartment because my job cut hours, my grandma, my kids and I had to stay in a hotel suite for about two weeks before our apartment was ready. Once my apartment was ready, I moved and started to get my life back on track. I continued to work until after I had my third child. I took about 4 months off then I went back to the job that I was on. Now I had three children and a grandmother to care for and yes it was hard, my grandmother was on dialysis which meant that she had lost her kidney and had to be connected to a machine 3 times a week to filter her blood, so her body could still function like she had a kidney. It was a struggle for me because she stayed sick a lot, sometimes in the middle of the night I would have to take her to the ER because of pain and then still had manage to make it to my job the next morning.

At the time, my third child's father was there to help me with the load of responsibilities that I had to handle, he worked at night and I worked during the day, so my grandma would always have someone there. That process went on for about another year then one day I woke up and it felt like I did not have a purpose. I was just working and caring for my family, I prayed and asked God to help me. I knew this was not what I wanted in my life, I wanted so much more.

I asked God to make me a stay at home mom because I was tired of working and working and yet I wasn't making any significant progress in life. Another year passed and one day I went to work, and my boss told everyone that the company was laying off people because the contract was ending, and the company was going out of business and we had a few months left. Remember I asked God to make me a stay at home mom, He did, you know after I got laid off from the job, I became a stay at home mom. A month before I got laid off, my grandma passed away. It was the worst turning point in my entire life. Grandma meant everything to me. The loss of my grandma was such a devastating process for me. I tried to keep it together because I had my children to care for at the time. A few months after that I was still grieving so I decided to get my mind occupied with something. I enrolled in a Psychiatric school in order to further my education. Right from high school, my dream has always been to become a beautician and a psychiatrist because I enjoyed listening to people helping them solve their problems. I used to say things and it would happen just as I had said it. It was a gift God gave me. I attended the psychiatric school for a few months and I really enjoyed it, it took my mind off a lot of emotions and helped me regain my focus and momentum. I went back to God and requested for a house for me and kids to live in. Before coming to the city, I always lived in a house. But since I came to the city, I have been living in apartments and it was a bit difficult for me because I wasn't used to people living that close to me.

A few months into going to school I met this guy and we started hanging out. His lifestyle was quite different from what I was accustom to, but I really enjoyed his company and the excitement of the things he was doing. He was a street guy. After dating him for a few months, his lifestyle started to influence me greatly and I stopped going to school and started hanging out with him a lot. Big mistake. This went on for about 9 more months and I found myself in another deep mess. I lost my apartment and ended up in a one-bedroom apartment with him and my 3 children. A few months later he went to jail and I became homeless. It was a really bad situation. I sent my 2 older kids to stay with my mom, she lived across town. I needed to figure out what I was going to do with my life. My baby was 2 years old at the time and we lived in a vacant apartment for 30 days. I should have been depressed but through that situation God sent people into my life to encourage me. I would pray to God every day, even though I was homeless, I still believed that God had more for me in this life. After the 30 days expired, I moved in with my mom and my 2 other children, this happened in November 2006. During that time, I started to seek God desperately to fill that void that I had in my heart, from missing my grandma to being homeless and then losing everything. I was mediating and seeking God daily while the kids were at school and my mom was working, so I had a lot of time to be alone with God. Time went by and I started to feel better and my hope in life was restored. I began planning to get a job and apartment.

I searched everywhere for jobs, filled out applications and everything but still no job. By March I was getting very frustrated about the way I was living and the fact that I didn't have a job, One day, my mom's boyfriend who lived there with us started harassing me and telling me I needed to get out because he was tired of listening to church talk. Actually, I paid my own portion of the bills with the check I got from my child support, so it was not about the money I believe it was my time to leave there.

I started praying to God to help me and my children get a place of our own, I thought about Abraham in the bible and when God told him to move me far away from his family. Remember I had told God the prior year that I wanted a house for me and the children. One day, I went to the mailbox and received a letter from a Section 8 program that was in small town outside of Dallas, Tx. They said that my name came up on the list, so the kids and I moved out from there with just bags of clothes. See when you ask God for stuff, he will give you what you asked for so ensure that you are specific in your asking. Yes, I got blessed with a house and did not have to pay for rent and I praised God so much for it. I failed to mention earlier when I first moved to Dallas, my mom and entire family moved in to stay with me on and off until they got on their feet. I never would turn my family down that needed my help and I never charged them a dime for rent. Little did I know that what you sow you would reap, years later God set me up to get a free house for me and my children and did not have to pay rent.

God spoke to me and said, "you let other people live rent free and never did you mishandle any one of them now it's your time to not have to pay rent." I learnt two major lessons during that whole transition in my life. Firstly, ensure that you are very specific when making a request from God, and secondly, God will reward you even if the people you helped fail to reward you. So now I was all alone in a town where I knew nobody. But I had asked God to move me far away from my family and he did just that. Always make your request plain with God. I did not have a car because my ex-boyfriend that went to jail got my car impounded and I did not have the money at the time to get it, so I had to let it go. My mom got me a car from one of our family members, let me just say it was a whoop-T. It got me from point A to point B. One day I woke up and started driving around looking for a church to attend and then I came across this church called the Holy Temple, shout out to the Lee Family.

I went to church that Sunday and after the service I went and spoke with the first lady of the church and explained my situation and before I could get home the church filled my 3-bedroom and 2 bath houses with everything I needed. The house that I was living in was only 7 years old at the time, a very nice house for me and my children. The church filled each room with beds and furniture I mean this stuff was nearly new, at that moment I knew I was where God wanted me. The next Sunday I went back to church and a lady by the name Ruthie Black came up to me and said I want to adopt you and your kids in my life.

Psalms 27:10—When my father and mother forsake me, Then Jehovah will take me up. When you think that no one cares and sees your pain God will place people in your life. Mrs. Black "granny" we called her she helped me and my children a lot and she reminded me a lot about my grandma and that really made me feel at home. Granny had a girlfriend; her best friend. Her name was Dorothy Brown and we all attended church together. I got to know this Mrs. Brown and she was like a mother figure in my life. She guided me on how to become a better mother. At the time, I was in my 20's and still not educated on being a mother so I needed guidance on how to be a good mother. God placed another grandmother and mother in my life to help me both spiritually and mentally to become the woman I am today. Still today, those 2 ladies are still in my life. I had to live out there for a year before I could move again. Once my year was up, I moved back to Dallas into another beautiful home. This program Section 8 was knew to me, so I had to learn a lot about how it worked. God led me to a house that did not take Section 8 or let me say that did not know about the program, the landlord wanted both the first and last month rent. But I only had half the money because I had to pay for another car God blessed me with after my whoop-t broke down. When I moved in that house on the outside Dallas, I got a new job that I drove 2 hours to work everyday and my car broke down one day and I could not get back home until I fixed my car. It took half of my deposit to fix my car.

Now God showed me favor, the landlord said "I do not know why I'm doing this and other people have all their money now, but I'm going to let you have the house and we will work out a payment plan for the restof the deposit".

I knew that was nothing but God moving for me. I had moved back to Dallas, but school was not out yet, so I had to let my 2 older kids stay with granny for 3 weeks until school was over for the year. I didn't want to take them out of school. A few months later the #street guy returned home from prison and we hooked back up, I was not waiting for him to get out and I was not dating while I lived out there, I was broke and in transition. I wasn't looking for a man at the time. When you are rebuilding your life, certain things do not matter and having a man at that time did not matter. I wanted to be financially stable and looking at a man was not going to help. A few months after moving back to Dallas the guy came around and we hooked back up. A very bad decision. We dated for 1 year and here comes my 4th child, we did not live together because he was a street guy and he stayed in the streets all the time. After I had our daughter one month later, he was back in jail. At that time, I made up my mind that I was done getting into relationships the wrong men. He was only supposed to be in my life for a season, but I kept him around. When I first met him, he helped me through my grieving process with my grandmother. He understood my situation at that time. You see, keeping people in your life when God has told you to let them go can mess up your life. I let that man back in my life and he almost destroyed my whole life and almost went to jail, but God saved me from the danger.

MY STORY

Now I had four children, no career and was still broke. The following summer I was sitting on my patio and was looking at my children playing in the back yard and tears started to run down my face like

a running faucet. The reason I was crying was because I put my children in my struggle. They did not ask to be here regardless of how they got here. I then looked up and asked God to forgive me for putting my children in a struggle that I did not want for myself. So right then my whole life changed, I went into my house and got on my laptop to find a school somewhere I could educate myself. I thought that if I go to college and got a degree, I could start making a better living for my family. I enrolled in private college the next week and started on my journey. A year later, that school could not fulfill what I needed so I enrolled in a community college and continued my journey. I wanted to major in education, so I could be a counselor at a school and help as many children as I could. That same year I enrolled into school, I went back to God with some more dreams- I said ok God you made me a stay at home mom like I asked, you gave me a house like I ask but God I'm broke, and I want to be financially stable. I asked God to give me an idea to make money and a door opened for me. A tax school was training people for 3 weeks on how to do taxes for free. I attended the training for 3 weeks and they basically showed me what I should do and not do so I took that and ran with it. The next year, I had my own tax business and I still was in school and also a stay at home mom.

After being in college for about 3 years, I figured I was going in the wrong direction by pursuing an education degree. I felt I needed a business degree because I was starting my first business, so I had to change my major. Just one year after I changed my major, I realized then that I did not necessarily need a degree in business to be an entrepreneur. After I had set up my business successfully, I then went out and got a job, so I could make more money. I worked on that job for a year and realized that I wanted and needed more, so I went back full time into my business until I found a higher paying job.

I got hired with a fortune 500 company with no degree. At the time, all my children where in school so a corporate job was not a problem. I also had a support system to help with the kids while I was at work in case something came up. I continued with my corporate job for about 3 years and I made good money. I even had 2 promotions while I was there. Once again when you're a born entrepreneur, you will find that working for other people will not sit well with you deep down in your spirit. That was how I felt at that time. This is my theory for working for someone else "They are paying you to make them rich and I can pay myself and make myself rich" After this occurred to me, I never went back to work for anyone else. I threw myself fully into entrepreneurship and started educating myself on business, marketing, branding and other things that would help me to become a successful business owner. While I was on Section 8, I took full advantage of the program while I had help because I know one thing free stuff does not last forever. Being on Section 8 gave me a chance to be at stay at home mother, go to college and started my own business. We never know how God will bless us even if it's through the government, so do not feel bad if you are on the government system. Remember the system is there to help you along your journey and will not last forever. While you are on the system get you a plan together to better yourself and your life. Everyone on this earth has a purpose and have gifts and talents. When you figure out your purpose and gifts you can profit from them. You do not have to go to college for your gifts and talents God placed within you. When I found my purpose, everything started to fall in place in my life. Take a journey back when you were young what did you enjoy doing a lot. Your purpose will always be connected to serving people at some compacity, examples are motivating, encouraging, teaching etc. Your talents are something that you have a passion for doing, example cooking, singing, drawing etc. When you find out your purpose, gifts and talents that's when your life will start to make since, and you will start to live on purpose and not just exist on earth.

Through my whole life, I noticed that I never gave up regardless of what life threw at me. I have had some tough knock down moments that made me hit my knees, but the thought of my children kept me going to be honest. When life takes you down to the point where you want to give up, you must look at the people that are counting on you knowing that if you fail they fail, and you don't want someone's else failure on your hands because you were too selfish to get up and try again. When you have children, you are their hero, they want to be like you. I could have given up and dropped out of school when I got pregnant. I could have given up after my grandmother died because my children would have felt the pain I felt when I lost someone. In this book, my intention is to show you that if I can make it then you too can overcome anything in life if you set your mind to it. You've read my story and I have overcome a lot of things in my past and I made it as a single parent of 4 children with no parental guidance and yet I still managed to be a successful woman and mother. With no help from my children fathers and no help from family members.

The reason I named my book From a Poverty mindset to a Wealthy mindset is because everyone's poverty is not the same. My bottom may not seem like a bottom to some people but that's where I started from. My main point is "believe in something if not you will fall for anything". That is my mindset. Some people think wealth is always money, but you can have a whole lot of money and have cancer or some diseases that keeps you from enjoying life. Wealth is way more than a person can imagine. You can be poor and be wealthy, that just means that everything that you need and want is available and you have peace about life. Remember Proverbs 18:21 "Life and death are in the power of your tongue". What you say comes to pass, so call wealth into your life because it covers all areas of your life. I have some chapters that will help you regardless of where you are at in life. Your help has arrived so let's get started on a new you. Living your best life with no apologies.

Things that I had to overcome through my journey.

1. Born into Poverty--- I MADE IT
2. Teen mother---- I MADE IT
3. Black sheep----- I MADE IT
4. Single mother of 4----- I MADE IT
5. Death of Grandmother------ I MADE IT
6. On Welfare---- I MADE IT
7. Depression---- I MADE IT
8. Broken- hearted----- I MADE IT
9. No Motherly or Fatherly Guidance---- I MADE IT

10. Being Broke no money------- I MADE IT
11. No College degree------ I MADE IT

WHAT IS POVERTY

Poverty is the state of one who lacks a certain amount of material possessions or money. Absolute poverty or destitution refers to the deprivation of basic human needs, which commonly includes food, water, sanitation, clothing, shelter, health care and education. Poverty can be a generational curse. Which means that you are in bondage of something, examples; bondage in an abusive relationship, bondage in finances, bondage with your body, bondage with disrespectful children, bondage with low self-esteem. Their all types of poverty which people do not realize, and everyone is facing some type of poverty somewhere in life. Some people do not understand that you can have poverty in the mind which is the lack of education or resources that you need to understand and comprehend life's decisions. If your mind is not in the state of making wise decisions, which is no wisdom, wisdom means the quality of having experience, knowledge, and good judgment. When you do the same thing over and over, the result is the same and that's because you still have a poverty mindset. Once you notice that you are getting the same results, then you have to renew your mind and educate yourself through reading books, seminars, conferences or whatever method is most suitable for you to get some kmowledge about the situation you are in and learn what you need to know and do to overcome it. Do not be captive to your mind. Whatever you read, watch, listen to or hang around that's what you will so start to imitate and become. So, watch what you read, watch, listen to and hang around; spirits are attachable.

WHAT IS WEALTH

Wealth is an abundance of valuable material possessions or resources. Wealth is not all about the material possessions because you can have all the money, houses and cars in the world but if your health is poor then you cannot enjoy that wealth of material things. True wealth is having the best healthy life you can have spiritually, mentally, emotionally, physically and financially. You can have a life that is rich in spirit which means that you are connected and have a relationship with God. Rich mentally is knowing how to make wise decisions when it comes to business and promotions. Rich emotionally knowing how to handle your emotions in all situations thinking before you clap back. Rich physically keeping your health as topmost priority know how to eat, what to eat and getting some type of exercise daily. Rich financially knowing how to be a good steward over money you have earned and not live a life you cannot afford to live. Matthew 16:26-- What good will it be for someone to gain the whole world, yet forfeit their soul? Ecclesiastes 10:19 -- Men prepare a meal for enjoyment, and wine makes life merry, and money is the answer to everything.

CONFIDENCE

Confidence means a feeling or consciousness of one's powers or of reliance on one's circumstances, faith or belief that one will act in a right, proper, or effective way. Do you know what kind of power you possess? Jeremiah 1:5 --I knew you before I formed you in your mother's womb. Before you were born, I set you apart and appointed you as my prophet to the nations. That scripture communicates that God set you apart from everyone else and made you a unique person. No one else has your powers. When a person has no confidence, it means that person has low self-esteem in an area. Along the way somewhere in your life, someone talked down to you, maybe told you were dumb, stupid, ugly, not going to be anything, you're too fat or skinny, no one will like you or whatever. Someone said something to you or done something that made you feel less than yourself, and that is where your confidence started to go down. The scripture above says that God set you apart which means that no one can play you like you can play you. This is your script (body, mind and soul), why would you allow another spirit to tell you that your creator made a mistake. Do you know who you are? What makes you? What does others like about your uniqueness? Those are the questions that you need to ask yourself. What traits set you apart? for instance, are you friendly, funny, silly, smart, sharp, witty, outgoing, life of the party, loving, etc. If you still are not sure of the qualities that makes you unique, then you should ask some of your family and friends. Find out what they like most about you, they will tell you somethings that makes you unique that you probably did not know. This is all about finding out who you are as a person apart from the titles you have. I want to know you without your titles such as mother, daughter, sister, lover, friend, businesswoman or all the degrees you have. When you do not have confidence or do not know your power that means that you let people control your soul; your soul is -your mind, will and emotion.

How will you allow someone else to take your power that God gave you? Everyone has their own power. You must look in the mirror and say I love everything about myself, even if you don't not feel it now. Proverbs 18:21: Death and life are in the power of the tongue: and they that love it shall eat the fruit thereof. If you cannot say nice things about yourself, then sit down get a piece of paper and write down everything that you do not like about yourself then start working on those things, so you can learn to love yourself better. Also ask God to take the scales off your eyes so that you can see yourself like he sees you. You only get one body you can always transform your mind to think differently and get different results. Please do not think surgery is a way out if you do not like your outwards appearance. God is saying that those things that you call your flaws are the things that makes you unique. You may have a big nose, big eyes, short hair, etc.; but those things there is what people like about you, because it is unique. When people have plastic surgery it looks and sounds good but at what cost? Many women suffer emotionally and physically behind those surgeries, and they have multiple problems afterwards. Big butts are great. However, most people have serious problems after those surgeries just to look good. They suffer back pain and stomach pain including all the meds they must take to help with the pain. I'm not against it but fix your mindset mentally, spiritually and emotionally. Surgery doesn't fix depression; it only makes the outside wrapping look pretty. That's like getting a beautifully wrapped gift only to find out that inside is dirty underwear, even though the wrapping was pretty. Be careful about covering up dirty inside your heart. Clean up your mind first and then work on your outer side. Psalm 139:14-- I praise you, for I am fearfully and wonderfully made. Wonderful are your works; my soul knows it very well.

If the bible says that you are fearfully and wonderfully made, why would you allow someone else or even yourself to convince you that you are not wonderfully made. Never allow what people say or think to affect you. You should remain fearless and confident in who God created. Genesis 1:31 And God saw everything that he had made, and, behold, it was very good.

Take your power back, other people's opinion matters less at this point in your life. You are only permitted to listen to people who are committed to helping you live your best live. Those are the ones whose opinions should matter. On judgement day, when you appear before your creator, he is not going to ask you about other people, but how you served his kingdom. He will not ask you about your parents, kids, husbands, friends etc. the only thing that God will be concerned with is if you fulfilled his purpose on earth. Remember that you are only answerable to God about how you live on earth. What other people did or said won't matter to him? You should be more concerned about your own salvation and not worry about whether other people would accept or like you. Since God has accepted you, forget about what other people have to say and be happy with yourself. Accept yourself the way you are and stop comparing yourself to others. When you compare yourself to others that is when you become a hater and then jealous will kick in. 3 John 1:11 Beloved, follow not that which is evil, but that which is good. He that doeth good is of God: but he that doeth evil hath not seen God. Do not worry about why you did not receive for was not made like someone else. God did not give you a big butt because he knew that you would have used it in the wrong way to fulfill your selfish desires which could have destroy you in the end, thereby failing to fulfill his purpose for you on this earth. God did not give you big breast because you would not want to cover your cleavage and would be violated by the wrong men. Be happy with the body that God gave you, which is His temple, once you destroy it, you will have to leave this earth (i.e death). God will not give you another body if you screw this one up. It does not work that way. Take care of the temple that God has given you and don't be jealous of other people's body, mind or spirit. Never want someone else's life because you do not know what they had to go through to have what they have, be careful of comparison. You see these women on T.V all the time with those model bodies, they are usually most of them are miserable and have insecurities and searching for attention. Some of those ladies on social media and on T.V. are on contracts and have to maintain the weight and looks in order to do business or vice versa that they need to change in order to get a contract. When someone tells you that they want you to change the way you look, run that is the devil's money all money is not good money. You will continue to make changes in order to be accepted.

Basically, they are telling you that they don't like the way God made you and that you need to change it so that you can be famous. Is losing your mind because of depression worth the fame? A lot of famous people are on drugs and committing suicide because they were told that they were not good enough and need to change something. Do not let society dictate you and take over your power. Be happy with the body and mind God gave you because that's your power and even if other people don't like it, God will send someone to you that loves you the way you are. You can never tell, what you have been looking for will come to you just because you stood up for yourself and loved yourself just as God made you. Never give up your power, because you are the only one God created that way. You are totally unique. Everyone came to this earth with a unique gift, talent and skills, just discover yours and develop it, then God's blessings will come on you because you know who you are I will leave you with this; Love who you are and embrace your uniqueness. When you start seeing yourself as complete, then people will look at you that way. What you put out confidently is what people will embrace. There is only one of your kind in this life, no one else can do the things you were designed to do because they are not equipped to handle them. Love yourself, because if you don't know one else will. Once you know who you are then you can discover what you need and the skills you should acquire for you to live your best life. The moral of the story is that you should not let anyone, or anything affect your confidence and the love you have for yourself. Because without it, you won't be able to live your best life. If you do not know who you are this is how you find yourself, you follow God and you will find yourself. Mathew 10:39 He that findeth his life shall lose it: and he that loseth his life for my sake shall find it. Philippian 1:6 For I am confident of this very thing, that He who began a good work in you will perfect it until the day of Christ Jesus. Philippian 4:13 I can do all things through Him who strengthens me.

Things a Confident Woman Needs to Have

1. Have a pray life
2. Have a mediation or quiet time everyday
3. Spend time working on something productive

CONFIDENCE

4. Give back- do something for someone else that needs help.

5. Exercise at least 30 minutes a day- walk, run, download a 7-minute workout video from YouTube.

6. Get a Mentor that can mentor you in your life

7. Set boundaries and do not settle for less.

8. Read something that will stimulate your mind- a church sermon, a life coach or from any other source that can build your self-worth (free on YouTube)

9. Know your purpose and full fill your destiny

10. Stay focused on your best life and what you need to do to accomplish your set goals

11. Find new friends who are already where you are going in life. If you want to be a millionaire, find where they hang out and go there, you will meet someone.

12. Find a hobby that helps you relax your mind

13. Find out what you really want in life

14. Change your wardrobe to match where you're going

15. Change your hairstyle

16. Change your nail color

17. Go to a restaurant that you've never been to before

18. Buy yourself something that you would normally not get for yourself- if shop at the thrift store go to JC Penny and buy something for yourself.

19. Change your room and get it organized, buy some nice and comfortable sheets so you can rest at night peacefully

20. At night write down a to do list for the next day

21. Get a calendar and start setting schedules for the week. Just make sure you are organized

22. Stay positive. People and situations will get on your nerves but just take a deep breath and stay focused. It's only a distraction—STAY FOCUSED

BROKEN PEOPLE

Broken means- damaged, no longer in one piece or working order. It also means giving up all hope, defeated, or beaten.

Are you broken or just pissed off, frustrated, angry or bitter because someone or something didn't do what you expected they should have done?

When you feel broken, its usually because someone did not meet up with what you expected from them. People will show you red flags when they do not want you, love you, or need you like you need them. Ignoring red flags will leave you hurt at the end.

Remember no one can break you if you don't allow it to happen. Most times God shows us red flags, but we ignore them and then we go ahead to complain that people have broken us. They did not break you, they only failed to meet your expectation and probably hurt your feelings which are your emotions. You might have expected that man or woman should love you in a certain way, but maybe that person did not have what it takes to love in that capacity. Some people can not love you the way you want them to. Some people will only love you the best way that they knew how to love.

Stop blaming people when you feel broken hearted, just recognize that you failed to see or ignored the red flags that they have showed you. Other people cannot break your heart or mind because you have control over that part of your body. People break what they have control over, if someone can break your heart then that person have control over your heart.

Blaming others because you got played, pimped, lied to, cheated on, rejected, abused, talked about etc. People will only treat you the way you allow them to treat you. People can only break you when you are already a broken vessel looking for someone to fix your inner needs. Get in tune with yourself, know your worth, how you want to be treated and how you want to feel. When you know these things, it will be hard for someone to come in and break you.

Here's my story of how I thought I was broken but really, I ignored all the red flags. I was in an eight-year old relationship with a guy who broke my heart. The guy and I never lived under the same roof because I had kids and would not allow men over my kids. But this guy did not want kids around as well because his kids were grown and he never lived with his own kids, red flag #1. We had a great friendship we could talk all-day about everything, so I kept it going with him. I was 100% into the relationship but the thing about the relationship was that the guy was a street guy and I was a Christian believer, red flag #2. We never spent any holidays together because Holidays was not his thing he proclaimed, red flag #3, This went on and on for years, but I was so into my kids and starting my business, I did miss out on a lot things. But believe me I was not a Fool all the way just in trying to love the wrong guy. I was getting myself into the position for the future that I was envisioning for my family. I went to college and started educating myself because I wanted more out of life and I knew that no one will take care of my kids and I, so I started the process. I started a business a year after me and this guy got together, and I kept going. I know that when you love someone a lot, you tend to be blind to the negative things about that person. The guy had so much potential, but our visions were different, red flag #4. I was envisioning a six-bedroom house and he was satisfied with a two-bedroom apartment. I knew then that our dreams were not going to fit together. He believed in God and he believed in the thought of God. On the other hand, I had a relationship with God. I am prayer, giver and faster but he did not believe in any of that, red flag #5. We were unequally yoked, *2 Corinthians* 6:14 Do not be unequally yoked together with unbelievers. How can righteousness be a partner with the wickedness? How can light live with darkness.

Ephesians 5:7 Therefore do not become partners with them. These were some of the red flags that I saw but I still maintained the relationship. Before I got into this relationship, I had just gotten out of an emotional and physical abusive relationship. I felt that getting into another relationship will help me cope with the pain but on the contrary it was a total mess. This guy never ever once helped me and my kids with any bills or anything of that nature, another red flag #6 but I still stayed. Sometimes, God shows us the wrong behaviors in people so he can save us from getting hurt by them. But if we decide to maintain such relationships, we will eventually learn from the painful experience. I gave him so much mentally, emotionally, physically and financially. My involvement with him was so strong. I had prayed severally about it and had even spoken to some of my friends to pray for me so that the soul tie I had with the guy would be broken. What eventually led to the breakup of our relationship was him cheating on me. This guy took all that I was giving him for granted and was cheating on me. He even went ahead to say that he didn't see anything wrong with him cheating on me, but it was nothing sexually. After that cheating episode, I was so devasted and broken because I had invested so much time into that relationship. When someone is not good for you and you still stay, God will allow them to hurt you so bad to make you leave them before they destroy you completely. For at least three months I was broken hearted and depressed, but I would listen to TD Jakes sermons all day every day to keep my sanity. I started calling psychics like I was crazy and letting them take my money just for them to tell me things that would never happen, I mean I thought I was going to lose my mind that some point. Then one of my spiritual brothers told me that those psychics practiced witchcraft and all they did was put evil spirits around me. So, I had to go to God and repent for that because my life was already in shambles. There is this quote that says to get over one, you must get under. So based on that mindset, I went into another relationship. At first, it was great because it helped me take my mind off all the pain, I had incurred for myself from my past relationship. Of course, that did not go well because I ended up going back to the same situation I was in before. One day, I made up my mind to get a handle of my emotions and regain my focus. I started seeking God, asking Him to heal and repair me so that my kids won't be affected by my emotional breakdown. I tried my best to hide it from them. God started showing me all the red flags in the relationship that I ignored. This guy was already broken as a person. He grew up with a mom that was on drugs and a father who spent most of his life in prison. So, he never had a childhood and therefore had no idea about what it meant for one to be loved and cherished. Despite all those red flags, I still stayed with him because I wanted to have a man in my life and that cost me a lot. It is wise to look up people's backgrounds before getting into a relationship with them. Backgrounds and DNA never lie, but if you chose them and all the baggage from childhood you cannot blame anyone but yourself. Remember, you cannot change people they have to want to change by themselves. You can encourage people, but that decision to change their habits can only be initiated by themselves. As a person you should understand what makes you feel loved at your core. My top core needs are quality time- a man must spend time with me even if he is in one room and I'm in another room it's his presence that makes me feel loved. second is words of affirmation- if you say you're going to do something please follow through, if you tell me you're going to mow the lawn, mow the lawn, if you say we are going somewhere I'm expecting to go somewhere- keep your word. These are the two major things a man must do to make me feel loved inside. However, this guy did not have any of these two qualities and that was the indication that he was not for me. Love languages are those core needs that should be in any relationship or friendship in other for you to feel loved and grow with each other. When you know what you need inside, then your choices for picking up mates for a relationship or friendship will become easier. This will help you to eliminate the broken people because broken people break people, remember that. Also, broken people hook up with other broke people. If you find yourself dating a broken person reality is that you are broken somewhere inside as well. Energies attract the same energy. That was one of the reasons that me and that guy stayed together so long because I was broken too deep down. Even though things did not work out between me and that guy and I got my feelings hurt, I still had to forgive myself for not paying attention to those red flags. It was not his fault, it was mine. He was my assignment from God, but I went another direction. A person who is an assignment from God is one whom you are meant to teach, coach or minister to. A spouse is a person that you can build with and have things to build with. I had to look at everything differently. When someone don't know who they are they will not recognize who you really are to them. Do not resist change when it is time to change. Once a person communicates to you that they do not mind if they break up with you, then you should leave that relationship first. Stop dragging people into your destiny, if they belong there, they will just show up. Never sow into people that are less than

BROKEN PEOPLE

you because when you need them, they will not deliver, and you will feel let down. When you're going through a difficult situation, find scriptures on that situation and meditate on them until you get peace. Don't let others break you-mentally, physically, financially or emotionally, that is not love that is Abuse. Would you hire someone without experience to work for you, if not stop hiring people who lack the experience to love you unless they are willing to be trained. We must be Replenished- Renewed and Refreshed daily. Ask God to renew you daily. Don't be on option, be a choice.

Being an Option puts you under probability of being chosen but when you are a Choice, you have been chosen already. You generally get what you expect, so expect to be happy. When you terminate someone from your life, stop giving them access through the same door you closed against them. When your done with someone, be done completely and never let them in again. Stop being available to pain, disrespect, abuse, and heartbreak. Ask yourself this question how can God get the glory out of this situation? God always finds purpose in dead things. If you believe, you will see the Glory of God. Stop focusing on the problem and focus on God's purpose for you. Hebrews 11:6 But without faith it is impossible to please him: for he that cometh to God must believe that he is, and that he is a rewarder of them that diligently seek him. If God delivered you based on your own terms, that means you do not need God, God is on his own time clock not on yours.

Whatever God called you to do, move on it. God is shaping you, and you can't follow God in the natural but in the spirit. Only God can do the supernatural miracles in people lives. Don't inherit someone else's problems. Cover your basis always talk to God about everything. If you can't wait on God, then you don't need it. Proverbs 29:18 Where there is no vision the people perish, but he that keepeth the law, happy is he. Consider the difficult situations as lessons that God has brought you out from both in the past and in present. If you're not being challenged, you cannot change. Learn to put childish things away. You can't change what you don't acknowledge. Some people need some type of counseling somewhere in their lives, either through mentorship programs, therapy, mentors or some type of guidance is necessary for us at some point in life to maintain our sanity. Counseling helps you understand who you are and to help you cope with other people differnces. It helps you relieve frustration, anger, hurt and anything else that is in the heart that needs to be release. If your team does not have God, then there is no team. Everyone needs mentors in all areas of their life to make it to the next level. Think about when you were in school all those teachers you needed just to teach you how to get to the next grade. A job has managers is to train you how to do the job that you were hired for. Having a team is very valuable as adult because we all need guidance and help with things in our life, mentally, physically, financially. In all those areas we need mentors to guide us. Ask God for direction and listen. You cannot put a nonperforming person in a performing position. As a leading lady, I am aware that most women that are loved are usually meek and humble. But most people may not be aware of this. Some talented people can perform well until a situation require more talent and that's when you find out who you really are. What type of person are you, Are you teachable? or do you always avoid the places that pushed you towards change? Do you need to make better choices to get a better outcome? Prepare for the change that you are asking God for. Get in position for change, meaning start changing things that you do, things you say and places you go. You must change what you use to depend on when it is disconnected. Until you change the page of a chapter you will continue doing what you are doing in relationships or friendships. Somethings must change in order to get a different result. You cannot change people's character. God must change their character. Watch what you say. The more you resist something; it will flee or go away. Change the way you speak and the way to understand things and you will get different results. It takes 30 days to change a story, keep saying positive things every day. John 10:10 The thief comes only to steal and kill and destroy; I have come that they may have life and have it to the full. A thief takes, hurts and leaves you. This is how you discover a thief (devil) in your life. God will never put you in a situation if he knew you could not make it, so do not get weary in well doing? Ask the Lord for the way forward; I've been hurt and abused, help me Lord to move forward, heal my heart. Change your attitude about your situation. God is making a message out of your mess. If God exposes you to something and it does not draw you, it's not for you. God's word is the foundation of your life- without a strong foundation. The devil attacks your heart if the devil can make you better you cannot be better. Look at the way a person dress and talk, the first impression will tell you a lot about a person. God said I cannot give you certain things right now because mentally you're not ready. Ask God for Wisdom and an understanding. If you want to know who you are, take a close look at your friends. Who do you feel comfortable around? Who do you call all the time? What do they having you doing? What do they have you listening too? What do they have you reading? Where do they have you going? What do they have you watching? What do they have you thinking about? How do they have you talking? What have they got you saying? How they got you feeling? Those are you questions to ask yourself about the people you bring into your life. It can be good or evil pay attention to who you let come into your life. Are you a luster or lover? A luster is wanting someone for what they have or what they can give you. A lover is loving someone unconditional even if they have nothing to give. Be disciplined. Are you choosing comfort over God? Slow down your mind and learn to process things that are happening in your life.

Take time to mature. Rest your weary soul, what is for you is for you. Get rooted in faith. When you believe, things change. What you believe will sustain you. When you are around people that are limited like you are, they compete with you do not complete you. Insecure jealous people will compete with you. If you have just left a relationship, give yourself time to heal? Figure out what went wrong in the relationship and how you played a role in the failed relationship. Seek God first. Matthew 6:33 King James Version (KJV). 33 But seek ye first the kingdom of God, and his righteousness; and all these things shall be added unto you. That scripture means praying to God daily about everything you are going through and for others and he will add all the things that you desire. We were created by God to serve God. Letting go is trusting God. Don't act out of anger act out of love. Ask God to heal your anger. Anger leads to hate. Release people that angers you. God knows who hurt you, but you go tell God how that made you feel and that you are depressed and sad, talk with God he is listening. You are God's daughter and he loves you and want to protect and love on you. Ask God to heal your heart then let go of the hurt, so God can heal you. Don't miss your blessing for being impatient. Don't be quick with your words. Watch what you say during your testing seasons in your life when you are really going through something. Don't give up so easily. Words come back when you send them out. God gives you wisdom to understand things. Your blessing may never appear the way you are expecting. It takes wisdom to do what you are called to do by God. God qualifies us, and no one can stop you. Open your eyes to the wisdom of the blessings of Change. Where are you going? Act like you're going somewhere. You're on your way somewhere. If you want to go somewhere change your circle of friends. Change the way you think. Put your angels to work stop doing what your angels are supposed to do for you. Hatred and anger blinds, they prevent you from seeing ahead. Your future is bright even if you are going through your darkest moment right now. You must go through the dark so that you can appreciate the light. Satan will make you curse your own blessing. You can be a Christian and be immature. A mature person will apologize even when they are right. Submit your plans before God- Lord is this your will for my plans? Stay humble when you are going through tough times, those experiences reveal your true character. When you can get even with your enemy and you chose not to, you have completely forgiven that person and just opened a spot so God can bless you. When you are broken inside, nothing will satisfy you. Some people are not attracted to you they are attracted to your spirit. Light attracts everything, Dark blocks everything. God wants you to learn from your mistakes and not be tied down by them. There is a purpose in your pain. I can handle it now- I'm growing in God's favor. Don't Judge the second half of your life by the first half. You had to lose your mind to change your mind. On your way to Gods favor expect things to get worse before they get better. Tell yourself this I'm ready now I got my priorities right, I know who I am and whose I am I know where I come from, I went through enough Hell. If someone can walk away easily then you did not really have them in the first place. Any love that does not continue was likely flawed in the first place. Do new things in your life to reduce the stress of life. If you are not willing to be tested God cannot use you, God sets up test so we can pass the test when we are in the storm. God will guide you through the storm. Whatever can walk away from you, you did not need it. God will not give you an undeveloped blessing. God blesses us according to our maturity. If you don't put heat or fire to something you will never know what it really is made of. You either Grow or Go. Transition yourself for a better you. Don't get stuck with people that are not moving. It's like running water. When water is stagnant, it becomes contaminated with bugs and debris. Inspect your circle of friends- you will become like the people you hang around. If you don't know what you need, you won't appreciate what God gives you. What you sow you shall reap. You can change what you reap by changing what you sow- If you want to reap friends, then you should be friendly, sow love and love will come, want money sow money. Sheltered by the Shepard that's God's protection. Ask God to renew your strength and joy through it all. If God allowed you to go through the storm, he knows that he has placed in you what it takes to come out of the storm. If you can live without a person that person is not who God sent to you. But if you feel like your life is incomplete without that person then that's your Rib God has for you.

You must look like a fool to become wise. The test is designed to challenge your weakness. If you're successful everywhere but here, it humbles you to pray. Lord I'm trusting you when I can't trace you. Positioning- Relocating yourself. Shifting- people leaving- shaking. Position correctly- open before Lord- Lord it's your will. People in your life either come up to the vision or move out your life. God says you can't get what you got if you don't see what I see. You get visions in your spirit before you get it in your life. Courage- It takes courage to be successful. Make up your mind and stick to it. When you must give up someone you really love God can bless you. What do you do? You got to learn a new you- what are you saying about you. Stop defining yourself of who you used to be. The more patience the gentler you will become. Act like a wife right now until God sends your husband. Practice for your spouse. Speak to God about your desires because, God will give you the desire of your heart. Don't let them play you, set your standards and leave them there. If you don't connect to someone then you can't communicate with them. Frustration comes when a person makes a mistake. A frustrated person will always flip the blame. When God promotes you, it will always be an escalation of trouble. It starts with your own people. When there is a hole in your character there's nothing that will satisfy you, love won't be enough. Being a leader- you're going to be watched by others a lot. You have more people that need you than who feeds you. Always eat on your level- if you can't afford steak eat chicken. One sided love if someone doesn't love you like you love them when they love you back, they will treat you any kind of way. It's not going to work.

Ask yourself why did I want this thing, for show or purpose? Position without a mission means driven by ego. Be mission driven. Until you know your mission, your resources will be denied. What you are praying for has a Why. Why do you want it? Anything that does not have a mission is abused. Storms come to test your foundation- your commitment as a Christian. How deep are your roots in God- If you don't have God's word in you, you can't fight Be grounded in God's word so when the storm comes you are ready. Ephesians 6:10-20. Finally, my brethren, be strong in the Lord and in the power of His might. Put on the whole armor of God, that you may be able to stand against the wiles of the devil. Therefore, take up the whole armor of God, that you may be able to withstand in the evil day, and having done all, to stand. Understand your mission. Maneuverer – how you got to where you're at now. God will shift you for your mission. Can you praise God in a pit? Praise God whenever everything is going wrong. If you don't know where you are- you don't know where you're going. New Season, New Order. Let the process began. Heal your heart. Don't go back to the pain. To have a different outcome in life you must make better choices in life. Dust yourself off and try again and do not let the pain or heartbreak from one person destroy you from finding love again. Remember not to ignore the red flags. I set out a plan, so you can dissect the situation and get yourself back on track.

Ask yourself these questions and let's start the healing process.

1. Why am I broken?
2. Who broke my heart/mind?
3. When did you become broken?
4. What made you feel broken?
5. How did you become broken?
6. What was your role in the mistake?
7. What made you get to the point that you wanted to change?

8. Reflect on what needs to change.

9. Write down what you want to change in your life.

10. Write your vision. (An ideal or a goal toward which one aspires, what do you want in life)

Red Flags to watch

1. **Prayer life**- if he does not have a relationship with God, he will not have a healthy relationship with you, and he cannot cover you when you are facing obstacles.

2. **How many kids does he has?** Some men have children are dealing with child support and that income will be taken from the home. How does he treats and takes care of his kids.

3. **How does he treat his mother?** If he does not have a healthy relationship with his mother, he will not have a healthy relationship with you.

4. **Character**- How does he serve other people, when you go out to eat how generous is, he in tipping the waiter or waitress.

5. **Substance/Provider**- What does he have to bring to the table, and does he want you to pay 50/50 on bills. Why should you help a man to help take care of you?

SLAVE MENTALITY

Slave means bondage, yoke, captive - a lot of people have a slave mind being held in bondage or lack. Some People think other people owe them something which is having a slave mentality no one owes anyone anything. Being held captive to the ways of your parents and grandparents. This is a new generation doing, saying and acting the way your parents or grandparents performed does not work for the new generation. What your parents went through doesn't mean you have to go through the same thing. The older generation was raised during slave, thought as a slave or was a slave owner. Even though they were free from slavery their minds were still in a slave mentality. Your parents and grandparent could only teach you from a slave mind because that is what they came from. They could not teach you from any other place but from a slave mind or enslaving someone else. They performed the best they could with what they knew and had at the time. Bondage means held against your will. When you change your mind frame you can get out of bondage. You can have what you want when you set your mind to see it. No one is getting 40 acres and a mule you have access to section 8 and food stamps. Just because your parents didn't go to school or own a home doesn't mean you can't do those things. It all depends on your choices. Get around people that are at a higher level in life than you, so you can watch and see how a successful person operates. The old saying "birds of a feather flock together," the people you surround yourself with will influence your habits. Having a slave mentality also comes when you say my momma did it and my grandma did it like that. But if you look at their lives and if it is not prosperous then you need to stop doing it like momma and grandma. In the black culture the parents are very heavy about beating their children, that

SLAVE MENTALITY

was a slave mentality that they took on from slavery when master used to beat the slaves in the fields when they would not do what they wanted them to do. So, master would roam the fields beating the slaves with belts and whips. The slaves started to do their children the same way the master did to the slaves in the cotton fields, when they did not do what they were told. We must do away with that slave mentality of beating children like slaves' verses displine the right way, because then the children become violent beaters themselves. Learn to communicate with them on why they did not follow direction, because you can beat a child and they still do the same thing that they were beaten for their action. Each time you beat a child, you give them the mindset that if someone does not do what they tell them to do you beat them.

Do not get me wrong it's okay to whip you child for being disobedient but not to the point of beating them unconscious. The phrase "spare the rod, spoil the child" is a modern-day proverb that means if a parent refuses to discipline an unruly child, that child will grow accustomed to getting his own way. He will become, in the common vernacular, a spoiled brat. The saying comes from Proverbs 13:24, "He who spares the rod hates his son, but he who loves him is careful to discipline him." The Lord uses discipline to reveal our sin to us. This is also how parents reveal the truth of our need for a Savior to their children. When a child does not feel the consequence of his sin, he will not understand that sin requires punishment. The Lord provides a way to salvation and forgiveness through Jesus, but that means little to those who do not see their sin. I remember growing up we would get beaten like we were in the cotton fields. I got beaten one time because I could not remember my birthday. That went on for hours and hours because I had ADHD when I was younger. Back then parents just thought kids did not want to learn, but that was not the case. When I was in school it would always take me longer to learn things so when I was being beaten for having a learning disability. But again, I was raised with slave mentality parents that they really did not understand a lot of things. Things that worked for our parents and grandparents does not always work for the new generation. Known what I know now about my learning disability I could never abuse my children into learning because I knew how that felt and how frustrating it was when really all wanted to do was learn but need extra help. As a parent our children are replica of us. When I saw that my first two children were having learn problems, I helped them more along with the teachers. I know first-hand how a child feels sitting in class and everyone around them is understanding what the teacher is teaching, and yet the child has no clue.

When a child is not comprehending what is being taught in class, they will become class clowns and start to disrupt the other students because their mindset is not understanding what is being taught. Children with those learning problems are usually the children that hate school, because they are not understanding or comprehending what the teacher is teaching. As parents we should not leave the obligation of teaching our children entirely to the teachers, it takes a village to raise children in this generation. I have four beautiful children the older two I worked a lot on a job when they were younger. They went to school and day care and that's who help raised them, I was young and did not know better because I was not around successful parents or women to learn how to raise my children. The first two of my children had the ADHD the learning disability like I did and was diagnosed with it. I know then my parenting skill had to kick in, so I would pray over them really all of them that this generational curse would be broken. The last two of my children are honor roll students and the reason they are honor roll students is because I spent more time with them as a stay at home mom. I did not send them off to the day care like the first two. I would read to them and teach them numbers, alphabet's, letters, basically everything that they needed to start school. Plus, I was going to college when my third child was in elementary and my baby was 1 year old. I was educating myself and so I started educating them as well. Before they both turned 3 years old, they knew their birthday, alphabets, numbers, colors, the basic kindergarten level. I look back at my children and see the difference between my two older children that the school and day care raised versus the two that I raised while I was a stay at home mom. There is a significant difference. Working moms work so hard to maintain a roof over their children's heads but then they miss out on raising their children which is the most key role as a mother. I know first-hand how hard the struggle is to provide for your children working, going to school, and all the activities that children want to do now days.

Not every woman can be a stay at home mom or would want to but what I am telling you, you must teach your children because they are your children. I took advantage of being a stay at home mom and revaluated my situation and wanted more for my life and theirs. I did not want to be stuck in a generational curse like my parents, so I started going to college and asked God to let me be financially stable, so I enrolled to a free tax training that lasted for three weeks at a tax school and they showed me the in and out so I started my own tax business. If you want a change bad enough you will get it, I did all these adventures on welfare yes welfare. Ladies if you are on the system and the government is helping you to be a stay at home parent and you are not teaching your children or helping them to be successful shame on you. Ladies come on out of that slave mentality. I was going to college and got paid to go over $19,000 per year tax free money. I received grant, loans and scholarships so that's how I took care of my family from one of my sources of incomes. I would put that money up and pay our bills. My children were well taken care of and did not want for anything. Other parents thought I was married for a long time because of how well I took care of my children and when they found out that I was a single parent with four children they could not believe it. See when you ask God for something get in position to receive it regardless of if its section 8, food stamps or any other government assistance, because those are blessings because everyone cannot receive government assist when they need it. You must have a plan if not you will fail. I have made some information available to help you set out a plan and get yourself out of this slave mentality because if you don't get out of slave mindset, then you will raise children with the same mindset that will soon have their children with the same slavery mindset. My first child seen some of my struggles I faced while raising them for example moving from apartment to apartment, I could not pay the rent, lights being off, just could not keep things moving in the right direction. I always worked but it seemed to never be enough. My second child vaguely remember those things thank God because children who we put in your struggles sometimes suffers later in life if you do not make a change for better and let them understand that you can go through a situation but do not let it brake you. Learning from struggles will teach you how to be strong in tough times and it will keep you humble. My last two children have never witnessed the struggle of lack and always thought I had it together. So those three children really do not know what a real struggle is and to be without. What made me want to change my life is when my last baby was 1 year old, and I was sitting on my patio one summer and my kids were playing in the back yard and I did not even have money to take my kids to the local pool. I looked up and said to God please forgive me for putting these innocent children into this struggle with tears running down my face. I said Lord show me what to do, that is when he told me to go to school, I jumped and went to my computer and started researching colleges. I found a school and made an appointment and started on my journey. When you set a goal for yourself and then draw up a plan to meet your goal, no one can stop you. A Dream written down with a date becomes a Goal, a goal broken down into steps becomes a Plan, a plan backed by Action becomes Reality. Question to ask yourself what is my Dream? It starts with you to make the change because those kids will grow up one day and all your children could remember is how they struggles growing up and they were not taught to dream and then go after your Dream. Parents that do not teach their children anything those parents are most likely to see their children make the same decision as they have. If you don't take care of your children, your children will not take care of you when you're older. These kids did not ask to come to this world so why would you treat them like they're in the way and not wanted because lack of knowledge on your behalf. Things that worked for our parents will not work for this generation of kids. Millennial kids are more expose to things that we were not exposed to. Social media is rising children right now so please let's get involved with our children because at the end of the day those are our future children. These children have more opportunities and advantages than what we had growing up, kids are savvier in technology than some parents. Let's stop this Slave Mentality curse now before we have a generation full of slave mentality children. Slave mentality is a generational curse and it must be broken somewhere. When people stop acting as if someone owes them something and go after their own dreams some of these curses will be broken. More than likely if your child sees you being successful, they will follow. Our kids do what they see and not all what you tell them. Remember that. The older generation would say do what I tell you to do and not what you see, that must have been one of the dumbest things a slave mentality person came up with. How will a kid do what you say and see you doing what you told them not to do that's been a hypocrite. Children do what we do, not all what we say. So, if you drink alcohol in front of your child and then tell them not to do that, really, how can you tell someone not to do something that you're doing in front of them. Do you see what I'm saying about the slavery mind? Parents lead by example whatever your child is doing is something they have observed you or someone do before. We are our children's first hero so don't be a lying hero that destroys a kid's mentality and confidence. Secondly, ensure you pay attention to the people and things around your environment because those factors can also affect your child's mentality. Just because you live in the hood doesn't mean you have to act that way.

That situation is just temporary so don't get comfortable being broke and disgusted. The reason why a lot of people are not successful is because of the company they keep. Putting all poor people together is never good because they cannot grow. When poor people live together their neighborhoods become Ghettos. Watch what you say because there is Power in your words. If you say you're broke you will stay broke, just say I'm in between blessings.

Run after your Destiny- find out what you love to do, what makes you smile when you do it. If you run after what's in front of you, you will not worry about what's behind you.

Even with your health. Most black people are used to eating unhealthy foods and we teach our children to do the same. If you observe from our ancestors, most of our them have health issues related to sugar diabetes, high blood, and obesity. They are teaching us how we will look and feel if we carry in their footsteps. Stay woke because it easy to carry on the slavery mentality, we must change our mind set. In this generations you can google any and everything we need in life so there is no excuse for the parents of this modern-day age. We must educate ourselves when we do not know things. Hosea 4:6 My people are destroyed for lack of knowledge: because thou hast rejected knowledge. The bible say that his people perish for the lack of knowledge. In all you are getting get a good understanding. Proverbs 4:7 Wisdom is the principal thing; therefore, get wisdom: and with all thy getting get understanding. If you do not know something google it, find people that know, find a book or get you a mentor. We as people should not be ignorant about anything when we have access to everything.

I'M TIRED OF MY KIDS

Have you said or have you heard someone say things like; I am tired of my kids, these kids make me sick, or I can't wait until these kids get grown? That does not mean that you're a bad parent because a lot of people have felt the same way at some point in time. You have a deeper reason why you say those things to your own children. Most parents that say these things have experienced some mental and emotional abuse from their parents. Somewhere down the line, their parents said those things to them when they were young. People that were loved and properly nurtured as children make better parents. When a child receives adequate attention from a parent, the child is more likely to respect and love their parent more. When a child hears a parent say that they are tired of them, it makes the child feels unwanted from the parent that brought them into this world. If your parents do not want you, who will. That is called Rejection, rejection means refusal to accept, submit to, believe, or make use of. No one wants to feel rejected because that makes you feel you're not good enough for anything and anybody. Children look up to their parents as heroes, children do what we do and not what we say. A child is formed when two people have sexual intercourse between two individuals where sperm passes from the male to the female's urethra. So that is a seed that has been passed through one body to another. Your spirit connects to your partner's spirit and then a soul is created. That means one spirit(parent) went through rejection, abandonment issues mental and physical abuse. The other spirit(parent) went through molestation, drug abuse, mental and physical abuse. When the spirits come together and make that soul that soul is being born with all that baggage from the past of both parents which is called generation curse that needs to be broken. This implies that parents are responsible for the character traits and mindsets that their children have. You must figure out what is the major reason why you are feeling like you are tired of your child.

What makes you tired of your children? Who made you have these children? Why do you want these children? What if your kids died today will you be happy then? Ask yourself those questions. No one wants to feel like they are in someone's way, do you know what it feels like to be rejected or live with the mindset that you are not accepted by your parents. We are going to change the way we feel about your children the bibles Psalm 127:3 Children are a blessing and a gift from the LORD That means that the children bless us, so if we have children God bless us with love, joy, peace, happiness and have life more abundantly. Stay woke most people are sleeping, everyone wants blessings and when God blessing you with something or someone you are still not happy. Luke 12:48 say When someone has been given much, much will be required in return; and when someone has been entrusted with much, even more will be required. God never said that we will not have to work to keep our blessings. If you don't work, you don't eat. Anything that you want, you must work for it, you get a house you must have a plan to pay for the house. Same with a car, if you get a car you will have to work to keep that car. As a husband or wife, you must work to keep your marriage. But when it comes to your children that is your own flesh and blood. You must learn to embrace your children while they are young, get involved with what they want to do in life. Ask them questions, talk with them, make them feel like you wished someone made you feel as a child. The more you get to know your child the more the child will get to know you. Tell your children about your life, that is how you get a bond with someone. Your child is a version of yourself so if you do not like yourself then you will probably not like your children. Raising a child can be tough sometimes, I know personally because I'm a single mother of four children. Ask God to show you how to love and enjoy you children. Talk to your children and let them know who you are and your life growing up as a child. Examples talk about your childhood who were your friends, what you did as kids for fun, what your school was like, what sports you played, how you use to dress, dance, how your parents treated you. Spend time with your children do activities with your children have a game night, take them to the $1 movies, go to the park. Just enjoy life with you children. Find something for your children to do and keep them busy, children love activities, color, painting, jump rope etc. When you keep children active, they will not get on your nerves. They are just bored and want your attention, give it to them because one day they will be grown and if you did not spend time with them, they will not want to spend time with you when they get older. Get to know your children while you can, and they get to know who you are as a person and parent. Remember what you say to your children because God loves us and whatever we are tired of God will take away from us so we can have some peace. The power of life and death are in the power of the tongue.

RENEW MY MIND

To achieve success in life despite all the pain and suffering that you have been through in your past. You must make up your mind to let go of the past and focus your attention on renewing your mind and start the process of living your best life. Romans 12:2-- Do not be conformed to the pattern of this world but be transformed by the renewing of your mind. Then you will be able to test and approve what God's will is--his good, pleasing and perfect will. Renewing your mind, you must let go of those things, people, and places that made you feel unhappy so you can achieve whatever your goals are in life. Do not let the world tell you who you are God said he made you fearful and wonderful being. You are unique and no one can take your power. When a person has taken your power, they have control over your mind. When you are depressed it means that you are refreshing a certain person, place or thing in your head over and over and this can go on for hours at time. That is the proof that whatever it is you are thinking of has power over your mind. Therefore, depressed people cannot move forward because all they think about is the problem and it hurts them over and over and over. When a person begins to have such an experience, it is very likely for suicide to set in because they feel that they cannot stop focusing on their problem. When you think about the problem to long that is when the pain starts to set inside of you, anxiety and panic attacks will start to manifest.

When you notice you are beginning to think about a situation for long periods of time, immediately refocus your attention and get rid of that thought or issue before you fall into depression. Here are some things that you can tell yourself when you start to focus on the situation for too long. Philippians 4:8--Fix your thoughts on what is true, and honorable, and right, and pure, and lovely, and admirable. Think about things that are excellent and worthy of praise. For example, when you notice your mind is back on that problem again, distract your mind by imagining how you will feel like if you were driving down the street in your dream car. Picture yourself driving down to your friend's place in your dream car. Imagine yourself in your dream house. Picture yourself lying on your beautiful bed and standing in your bathroom with very beautiful decorations and colors. How about thinking about planning your goals and achieving them so you can live your best life. Those are the thoughts you need to mediate on and not that negative situation. That is what the scripture is referring to when it says you should think on things that are lovely, pure, true, admirable, peaceful etc. When you renew your mind on new things then you start attracting new things. When you focus on a negative situation for so long in your mind, that situation becomes a strong hold and you must learn to bring it down. Ask yourself when you start to think on that situation, is this situation giving me peace or taking my peace. If it is taking your peace start thinking on the things you want to accomplish in your life. Many people are letting this type of situation steal their future of having and becoming the best person they can be. While you are focusing on that situation, other people are living their best life. Why would you want to keep making yourself sad and depressed about a situation? The best way to kill a dead situation is to start living your best life. When you start to live your best life, you will have found yourself so busy working on your goals and dreams that your mind is not on the situation anymore. We must practice every day of our life to get up and stay focused on our dreams. I know you will find yourself still thinking about the situation sometimes but Do Not stay there for long, whenever it comes to mind, take your focus back on things that are true, good and peaceful. Think about good things like you have eyes to see, you can talk and walk, you have all your limbs you can breathe, those are the things that we take for granted whereas someone wishes that they had something that we take for granted.

When you start to see how blessed you truly are then when those dead situations come up in your life you know how to handle that strong hold. We must renew our minds daily to stay focused and not faint. The scripture tells us in Ecclesiastes 9:11--The race is not to the swift or the battle to the strong, nor does food come to the wise or wealth to the brilliant or favor to the learned; but time and chance happen to them all. Everyone goes through times in life that they are in a storm and most people may never be aware. Here is a list of things that you can ask yourself and start to work on. When you have things to work on in your life you really do not have time to focus on dead situation. When you start to renew your mind, you will need mentors to help you? When you notice that your beginning to focus for too long on a situation, I start looking for people to minister, help and pray for to keep my mind fouced. I start to think about the positive things in life. AlsoI get on Social media and listen to Pastors sermons that would keep my mind focused. I would listen to sermon after sermon to keep my mind in check. That is also a form of mediating on the word. After I have listened to hours and hours of spiritual guidance, I notice that I have totally forgotten about that dead situation. God said seek him and you will find him. When I started to listen to sermon after sermon God was giving me so much wisdom. That is how God talks to us through people, places or things. It's from God when you can feel those words deep in your spirit and you then get a sense of peace over you. This is one of my favorite scriptures Matthew 6:33--But seek first the kingdom of God and his righteousness, and all these things will be added to you. Check out the list and answer those question and let's get a plan to fix your mind.

Ask yourself these questions below:

1. Why am I not happy?
2. Who is hindering me?
3. What do I want to be when I grow up?
4. Why do I think the way I do, who taught me?
5. I hate the way I look, what area?
6. I'm broke, Why?
7. I'm needy, Why?
8. What am I watching on T.V.?
9. What am I listening to on the radio?
10. Who do I confide in?

11. Who am I without my accomplishments?

12. Who do I want to be, the best me?

13. What's my vision (what do you want in life)

14. What is my best life and what does it look like?

15. What am I mediating on?

DATING WHILE RAISING KIDS

When single parents are raising children, they think that they must wait until their children are all grown before they can have a life which is not healthy for your own social life. When you are raising children, you can easily lose yourself. You will be so focused on your children that you might lose who you are as a person. So, I would advise that you can enjoy your life while raising your children so when your children are grown and doing their own thing you do not have to rediscover or start figuring out who you are as a person. I'm not talking about partying every chance you get to get away from your children every weekend. I would say a few times a month just relax and enjoy other adults. This is hard for some woman because they meet a man and want the man to move in with them and their children that is a big no, no not until you know that man can take care of you and those children. Having an adult life while raising your children will keep your life balanced so you will not be so obsessed with your children and you will still have a social life for yourself. Take some time out for yourself. Go out with friends, go on dates, just keep living. When you do start to date someone, always remember as a single parent that you are dating for you and your children. If the man like you then he will have to like your children if not, that is not the right man for you at the time. Let the man you are dating know how many children you have and if he is okay with that, then you can start to dig into his life and ask questions about his background like "where you raised by your father and mother?" If a man was not raised by a good father, he will most likely not know how to father your children. Ask him if he likes children or if he has children of his own. If he says that he does but he has not seen them or do not want to see them then that's probably not a guy for you and your children. How can a man not take care of his own flesh and blood and then you think he will take care of kids that are not his own children, think about that one? Before you can even consider dating someone you will need to make sure you know what you need inside your core. Those are your love languages. I will provide some details about that after this chapter so that you can have a guide that will help you identify your core needs before you begin to date any man or accept their request. Knowing your love languages will help prep you on what you need in order to feel loved by another person. Once you discover your love languages then you can start to date so you will not just date over and over and over and not find what you are looking for. Also, while dating and raising kids you never want to bring your date around your children until you both agree that you will be taking the friendship to a real relationship. When you decide to take it to the next level this is how you can tell that this man is serious with you. He will start helping you out financially before he even gets to meet the children. He will want to make sure your children are taking care of without asking where's their father and why he is not helping you. As a mother when a man cares for your children and want to make sure their fully taken care of regardless of whether their father is in the picture or not, this could be your man. Ask a lot of questions and watch his actions around your children because you do not want an undercover pedophile on your hands. Tips on a real man that has you and your children's best interest at hand, he will do and pay for things without you having to ask him for anything. Any real man that approaches you and finds out that you have children will may sure you and them kids are provided who. If he can take care of her children, then she knows he will take care of her. Ladies just be wise when dating and raising children because you do not want to bring the wrong person around your children and mess them up emotional, mentally and physically. Having a man in your bed is not worth it if your children will be affected in the long run. I would advise if the man is not talking let's get married then you do not need him in your bed or house at all. Children pay attention to those things and you do not want different men in and out your house you then teach your children how to be female whores and male whores. This should not take years and years for a man that wants you and the kids. After the man starts spending money on the kids, he will want to start spending time with the kids. I would allow him to meet the kids on outings like parks, restaurants, places kids can play just so you guys can see how things will work as a family. But never invite him to your house until you have gone to enough outings that the kids are comfortable with him around then he can start coming to the house. Let the kids warm up to him before you bring him in. The kids will then let you know if they like him or not, kid's discernment sometimes is stronger than ours because sometimes woman are looking for love and companionship so bad that we may miss out on things that is not right with the guy. Take hid when your children tell you about a man, once you lay down with a man your outlook on him changes because now your souls are tied, and you cannot see past the affection you have for that man. Let the man be around your friends or maybe a family member to see if they see something that you cannot see, if possible a male family member or friend so they can discern the new guy and they will tell you straight like it is from a man's point of view. If you are a woman that does not chose to date now that is ok to but make sure you stay socially connected with friends or family, so you can have that balanced life, so you will not get so overwhelmed with the stress of raising your children. Raising children alone is not all bad. You must learn to enjoy your children in that season because once they get to be teenagers, they will leave you behind and you will be at home lonely while the kids are out enjoying their lives. It's okay to be alone but not lonely. Being lonely will make you make decisions out of desperation for companionship. Learn to balance your life, make sure you are totally done with your children's father before you try to date because no man wants to come into a situation where you are always complaining about the children's father not helping and all. You should get over your breakup and stop blaming the man for all your problems. Rather, get busy with some work so that you can raise the children God has blessed you with. Your experience with this man should guide you in choosing a man when you want to date. When God separates you from your kid's father, it because He knows that them being around can mess your children up emotionally, mentally and physically. Stop begging for fathers to take care of your children, there is a reason why God keeps them away, remember that. Those are some tips if you want to date while raising kids because you do not want to let your children get grown and then leave you stuck trying to discover who you are and what you want in your life. It's harder when you are older to find a social life because the times has changed and you are out there looking dumb founded and not know where to start. Keep living your life, you are not dead because you have children. Enjoy your children and your own life. That is called living your best life within yourself because you did not lose yourself. If as a woman you notice that you have lost yourself, get up and start taking yourself out once a week by yourself, go to the movies, out to eat, somewhere you know that there are good quality men are cigar lounges even if you do not smoke, check out for men there. Go somewhere, get out of the house by yourself, no children. If you do not start now you will get so comfortable at being home bound, you will be scared to go outside just work and home. God wants us to enjoy our lives John 10:10--The thief comes only to steal and kill and destroy. I came that they may have life and have it abundantly. Live your abundant life because God said so, stop letting the devil steal your peace and enjoy life. Check out the website and find what your 5 love languages are and when you start to date if that person is not meeting those love languages then you should know that is not your guy. Keep dating because someone will meet at lease your top 3, do not waste your time if they are not meeting your core needs then it's not worth it, you should not have to teach the right person those things that you need it will just come naturally.

WHAT'S MY LOVE LANGUAGES

You can google online love languages and when you find your love languages- those are the things you need in a relationship to feel loved inside. Write them down below so you can keep them in plain sight so whenever you start to date someone, and they do not show you any of your listed core needs below do not waste your time. http://www.5lovelanguages.com

My 5 love languages

1. _____
2. _____
3. _____
4. _____
5. _____

MY FINANCES

Let's talk about your finances. Are you living from paycheck to paycheck and you want to be financially stable and want to live a comfortable life? Ask yourself are you happy at the job or business that you have at moment. If the answer is No, let's stop wasting time doing a job or business that you are not happy with doing. Luke 12:48--But someone who does not know, and then does something wrong, will be punished only lightly. When someone has been given much, much will be required in return; and when someone has been entrusted with much, even more will be required. First, you must figure out what level of finances you would like to operate from, like the scripture states much given much require meaning the more you want in life the harder you will have to work in order to achieve the success you are trying to achieve. Ask yourself how much money you would like to make in a year. Once you have discovered were you want to be financially, then you need to get a plan together. Are there things around your house that you are not using that you can sell? Are their extra bills that you need to eliminate or reduce at the time and start to save that money? Sometimes you must get rid of the old to make room for the new, if you have not used something within a year that means that you will not miss it if you sell it. How does your credit look now, pull your credit report you get a free credit report once a year? Having good credit will help you in the long run. When you need to apply for something, your interest rate will not be high, and you can save some money. If you credit is not over at least a 600 find you a credit repair person to help you with your credit. Credit repair persons are not that expensive you can get one as low as $35 per month. Just goggle credit repair or go on social media sights like Facebook, Instagram, Snapchat and search credit repair, it will be worth the investment. I had to repair my credit I went through Lexington Credit company so I could boost my credit score up. To be financially stable, you will have to be disciplined in your spending before you shop, ask yourself if it is a need or want. If it's a want then you do not need it at the time, but if you really want that item then you will have to sacrifice something else that you spend money on that you really do not have to have right now. We all have somethings that we can sell to make money, especially if you have children that outgrown their clothes fast. You can sell those clothes instead of dropping them off and lose money that you can use for something else important in your life. Instead of eating out on your lunch break, cook meals and take them to work. If you do not watch much T.V, do you really need cable or subscribe to the minimum package that they have to reduce you bill. When it comes to financial stability you will have to start to sacrifice things that you enjoy temporarily until you can get to your financial goal. Yes, this will be hard at the beginning like everything else in life, if you are used to spending and spending with no self-control, this will be a challenge, but life is a challenge. If you are tired of being Broke, then you will make the necessary moves to become debt free. Trust me you can do it when you set your mind to it and stick with the plan, I know sometimes you may back slide on spending but realize it and get back on track. Things come up in life unexpectedly and you may have to use the stash money but do not get frustrated that you had to go into the savings, just stay on the course and keep saving. We set financial goals so that in case emergencies arise, we do not have to worry about where to go borrow money from. Stay on course and it will pay off at the end. Spending less than want you earn. You must do what you have to do now, so you can do what you want to do later when your money is great. The goal is at least having 6 to 12 months of bills saved. That goal is a statistic goal for people who make the money and can afford to save a lot, but I understand when you are just making ends meet. Start with a goal that is realistic for you, instead try and save a $100 a month in a year that is $1200. That is a start and you must start somewhere to get to your desired goal one day. The point is to just get started somewhere at whatever level that you are at here in the moment. If your money is not where you want it to be you really do not have to fall for foolish games. You must be really focused on coming out of Poverty. All that clubbing or hanging out, you cannot afford that lifestyle on your budget right now, you can play later when you have your money together and really live you best life like traveling the world and seeing things that you have only dreamt of. When you want to go to the next level in your life, find people that are financially stable or get some books on money then sit, watch and learn from them, it will teach and motivate. When you are busy getting your life and money in order you will lose a lot of people along the way, friends and family. Some people will not understand the level you're on and yes, they will talk about you but right now you're not worried about who is not liking you when you are broke. Trust me you really want people out of your life that are not on the level you are trying to grow to because they will become a hinderance later. They will be basically full of jealous because you worked hard to be successful while they were doing nothing. The more you move up in life the more you will find yourself with less friends and family. When you are busy trying to be successful you do not have time for unserious people. Your attitude will determine how far you will make it in life. The only difference between you and a rich person is their attitude. You must condition your mind to get rich and not just look rich. Stop living someone else's dream and start living your own dream. When you are at your job, you are living someone else's dream. They dream that they would be rich and have people working for them, like some of us do now. Ask yourself what's your dream and let's start living it and make no apologies for it to no one. Also, once you have accomplished your goal stay on course and keep living within your means like you have been doing and you will see that you can live without some of those things and start living a better life. When dealing with finances you will have to be patient. Sacrifice, work hard, spend wisely, telling yourself no when your mind is saying yes, and focus on have the abundant life and not have to worry about money all the time so you can live your best life. You must do the work. The principle that I stood on from the bible that kept me knowledge about money was Malachi 3:10 Bring ye all the tithes into the storehouse, that there may be meat in mine house, and prove me now herewith, saith the Lord of hosts, if I will not open you the windows of heaven, and pour you out a blessing, that there shall not be room enough to receive it. Every time I would pay by tithes 10 percent of anything that God bless me with, my money never seemed to run out. God showed me how to spend on things and how to be a good steward of my money. I used to shop at thrift store for me and my children and saves all kinds of money. I would buy my work clothes from the thrift store and then take them to the cleaners and

MY FINANCES

have them cleaned and pressed down. People at my job taught that I had lots of money because I was always well dressed, and they did not even know I went to the thrift store. One time a lady that I was working with said she had seen a shirt I had on that came from Macy's that cost $150 dollars and I paid $5 for the thrift store. When you use wisdom, it will have you looking wealthy. Those are some of my money tips I done when I was trying to save some money. Check out the list below and see where you are with your finances. Let's see what we can change, remove or reduce to save some money. Make some changes for 6 months to a 1 year and see how it will change your life.

MY FINANCES

What is your cost of living Now?

These are your monthly expenses

Rent/Mortgage: _____

Electric: _____

Car Note: _____

Food: _____

Life Insurance: _____

Car Insurance: _____

Cable: _____

Internet: _____

Phone-Home: _____

Cell Phone: _____

Tithes: _____

House stuff Etc.: _____

Rental/Home Insurance: _____

Mortgage Taxes: _____

MY FINANCES

School Lunch: _____

Day Care: _____

Private School: _____

Hairstyle/Cut: _____

Rent/Mortgage: _____

Electric: _____

Car Note: _____

Food: _____

Life Insurance: _____

Car Insurance: _____

Cable: _____

Internet: _____

Phone-Home: _____

Cell Phone: _____

Tithes: _____   _____

House stuff Etc.: _____

Total: _____

Take the total of the bills above and (*multiply by 12) and that is your cost of living to maintain the lifestyle that you have now. So, if you have more bills than income that means you either must get another job or skill to make more money or discontinue/ reduce the bills above.

Example total: __$3585_ * 12= $43,020

If you have a job and your annual income is $48000 this difference is $4980 that you still have left over at the end of the year to save on each month.

So, if you make $38,500 a year you have a negative -$4,520 that you must come up with every month to make ends meet. That means that you have more bills than money. Some people would say your living outside you means but you just living paycheck to paycheck for the basic living. Now we should find a way to make extra income to make up the difference. God blessed us All with gifts and talents to do something very well, take that gift or talent and let's start making money on the side. Example of gifts and talents do you write well write a book, do you cook well sell dinner plates, do you do hair well set appointments, do you do make-up well find clients and do their make-up. Do you sing well get with event planners to be singers at events, do you like babysitting kids start a in home daycare or keep children on the weekends or late nights. What do you have passion to do and you love to do it?

After you have identified your recurrent expenses, you can now decide how much you should save each month from your income. Based on the kind of lifestyle you desire for yourself, you can then setup a savings plan that can help you achieve that lifestyle. Living your best life is not going to come over night, it is a process. Now what type of lifestyle would you like to have. Make you a vision board describing the type of house you want both the interior and exterior designs, what kind of car would you like to have, what type of vacations can you see yourself going on. What type of wedding do you want to have? What nonprofit organization would you will like to donate to because without a vision for yourself and helping others, your vision is selfish, and God will not bless a selfish person. Habakkuk 2:2 And the Lord answered me, and said, Write the vision, and make it plain upon tables, that he may run that breadth it. Write down all your dreams and goals and make it plain very plain what you need and want in life then set a plan or get a mentor to help achieve those goals. If you still think that you need for help with you finances, setup a one on one session and let's discuss you a financial plan for your life. You will find my website and other resources at the back of my book.

HOW TO COMMUNICATE WITH CHILDREN

When it comes to talking with your children? The main key is to listen to them regardless if you think and know that what they did or going to do. Never silence a child that teaches them that their voice does not matter, and they will learn to be closed adults and not know how to communicate later in life. Talk with them and not at them. Talk to a child on their level so they will understand what you are trying to teach and tell them. Children come into this world as a blank piece of paper, we teach them everything that they know. So therefore, children have not been here before in life, so we must treat them as such. Children do not understand nothing about bills and life we must teach them those things. The tone of your voice really plays a part on how a child will respond. Take a moment and reflect. When you were a child, how did you expect people to speak to you. You must learn to listen to your children to understand who they are as individuals and their feelings about things even if it is wrong or right. Be able to guide your children when they are wrong and show them what is right. If you cannot show a child where they are wrong, they will continue to assume that what they are doing is right. Make a child feel special and you can get a better relationship with them. Hugging and kissing your children shows them that you love them. Praise your children when they do good. Reward them with things when they are good. Parents are children's guides in life because we were once like them before, so we know what worked for us and what did not work for us. Build a bond and relationship with your children. Sit your children down and tell them about your childhood and how you grew up. Tell them about the challenges you faced in your household, talk about when you were in school, what sports, and activites that you participated in. Tell them what your hobbies and interest were growing up. Those are the things that help parents and children build strong relationships. Now a days, parents are raising children and when they grow up the parents are strangers to them because they never knew their parents background and how they grew up in life. Some things that we did as children, we will see it in our children. That is why it is very important to get a relationship with your children. Ask you children what they what to be when they grow up. Teach your children about God. Be an example to your children. Be good examples in front of your children. I'm not saying you cannot go about your adult lifestyle, just make sure your children are not around to see you do those things. Bringing different men and woman around your children is wrong, because if your children see that then they will grow up and have different men and woman around their children. Tell your children about the negative choices you made in your life so that they can avoid making those same decisions. We as parents made plenty mistakes but if you correct them, you become an example of a good parent. That way, you will help you children learn to get back up whenever they fail. Pray for your children daily to keep them covered. There is so much going on in the world and we are not around our children 24/7, so we need all the security necessary to protect our children. Children will listen if we learn to talk with them, they can understand what we say and mean. Believe me, children will act like they are not listen but when it comes down to what you told them they will quickly remember what you said. We must repeat things to them over and over until they receive it. Parents do not get frustrated because this is part of raising your children. Remember, our children are like smaller versions of ourselves. So, when you fight your children, you are fighting yourself because part of your DNA mixed with someone else's DNA formed a child. So, you should be careful of the person you choose to have children with because that person makes up half of your child. Children are the best teachers for parents, my children have taught me what love is, what patience is, what crazy means, how to multi task, what I was like growing up, not to lie, not to curse, that everything will be ok, etc. You can have a sad day but when you see your children's innocent faces all that negative thoughts leaves your mind; children give peace and calmness. Learn to love your children because one day they will be gone, and you will be all lone. How you treat you children when they are young that is the way they will treat you when you get old, remember that. The way you talk to your children when they are young that is how they will talk to you when they grow up. Respect your children and your children will respect you. The bible says train up a child in the way they should go. Proverbs 22:6 Train up a child in the way he should go: and when he is old, he will not depart from it. What you instill in your child will remain in them good or bad. Watch what seed you plant in your child because it will grow good or bad.

YOUR 18 GET OUT

I have heard this from many parents before, asking their children to leave their house once they turn 18. When your child turns 18, they are still children in their minds. Just sit back and think about it. How long did it take you to learn life and to become stable? How settled do you think they will be when they get to your age. As Parents, we must set our children up to be successful. When parents want their children out of the house at 18 that means that you taught and gave them the right knowledge and wisdom to make it out there on their own. Some parents are setting their children up for failure when they are not prepared mentally and financially. I completely understand that some childrens rebellionous will cause them to have to leave at 18 because they do not want o follow rules of the huse, Also when you get a child to be rebellious means they have some rooted issues that you do not know about and they will need therpery to find out what wrong inside for all the anger. When you show a child the struggles of life, like getting your lights cut off, not having food to feed them or not being able to send your child to school with decent clothes on. Children get bullied for the things that parents were unable to provide for them. Children should not have to worry about how they can go out and make money to help their parents with the bill that is a lot of pressure for a child to handle when their minds are not developed all the way. I know it can be hard sometimes and you do have to pull together as a family for a little bit but not the childs whole life of dependence as helping parents financially. Some young men have taken their fathers position in helping their mother financially because the father is absent of deceed. No child should ever wander into the streets because they are looking for a way to raise money for their parents. Children now a days have more drive an wisdom than some parents. Parents it's time to take responsibility for our children that we brought into this world. Even if the other parent is not around, that should motivate you even more not to let your children down again since the other parent already let them down. There are too many children raising parents because the parents have given up on life or became disabled or on drugs. Parents, I do understand some children are just out of hand and you will have to put them out if you choose too. Some children become disrespectful to parents that was there for them and the children are spoiled with love with no respect.

A child will show you signs early before the age of 18 that something is not right in their mind, that is when you should seek help for them at the with some type of counseling. Most schools offer free counseling services. Children can feel the pressure when a parent is going through tough times. As a parent, you should want better for your child than you had or prepare a foundation for your child, so they will not have to struggle through life. Children owe you what you gave them, and they will give you what you gave them when they grow up. When a child is 18 here are some of the things you should have taught them: Learn to put God first and foremost, How to cook, How to clean and manage a house, buying groceries, buying clothes, cars, houses, how to get a driver licenses or ID, applying for a job, applying for college, relationships, Insurance (life, auto), Credit scores, how to get a bank account and savings account, stocks and bonds investments, tithing, drugs, alcohol, sex, STD's, getting your physicals every year, visiting the dentist every year, choosing a career plans, college majors, being an entrepreneur, those are some of things that an 18 year should know before you kick them out. If you will not teach them, the streets will, and they will have a harder life which will not end up well. Parents if you do not know some of the things on the list to teach your child. You can only teach what you know, so if you are not educated about most of the things mention above, invest in yourself and get the relevant knowledge so that you too can teach your children the necessary things they need to know to get a head start in life or let someone else teach them the things that are needed to succeed in life. When you do so, you will reap a good reward from you children in future and God will also reward you.

Hosea 4:6-- My people are destroyed for lack of knowledge; because you have rejected knowledge, I reject you from being a priest to me. And since you have forgotten the law of your God, I also will forget your children. This scripture is very powerful. When you are teaching your children understand that God holds us accountable for teaching our children. If you are willing to learn, God will send you someone in your life to teach you or teach your child. But remember, you should lead by example. So, if you do not know something or have never done it, how can you teach or show your children. Your children will do what you do not what you always say. Proverbs 22:6--Train up a child in the way he should go; even when he is old, he will not depart from it. When you get ready to kick your child out read this scripture, if you have trained them with the essential needs that they should have, free them and let the fly. College is not for everyone. No one in the bible became very successful by going to college. Do not get me wrong college is good for certain careers doctors, lawyers, engineers' things in that nature. I would even go a step futher and say let your children to a 2-year community college to get the feel of the real world and learn the basics. When your children are in their teenage years watch them to see what their passions are because those are the talents and gifts that God has given them. When you learn what the gifts and talents are that your children possess that is when you start pulling that gift to the fore front. Example do they like to sing get them some singing classes, if its sports put them in extra sports, if it's doing hair get them some dolls to practice on. As a parent, that is one of our duties. To make sure that our children are successful adults in the world. I know some people will say I do not have the money to put them in certain programs like that, when God see that you are serious about your children passions, you pray to God to send the resources or the person that can help you birth out your childs gifts and talents. Trust me God will do just that, I remember when my son loves basketball and God knew that, one summer he went to a park to play basketball and a select team was practicing there, a select basketball team is a team outside of a school function that is a league by itself. They were practicing and the coach seen my son and ask him did he want to practice with them today. Of course, my son starting practicing with them and doing his thing that he knew best was balling. After the practice the coach brought my son home and asked could he be a part of the team, with select teams the parents must pay and it's not cheap. The coach said we want him on our team your son is very talented then he said the cost to start is $350 but all you pay is $50 for his uniform. See how God set that up, when you have a relationship with God your children are blessed too. I have a different parenting strategy than others. My children cannot move out of my home until they know their purpose on earth so that they will not just be wandering the world without purpose and direction. Working without a specific goal or vision. Another important thing is that my children must have at least two streams of income, that's how I'll know that they can be financially stable and will not have to call me saying they cannot pay their bills. I want to make sure that my children have what they need as adults to sustain the lifestyle that they are accustomed too. When my child fails because of inadequate training about the basics of life, then I failed them as a parent. If I do not know, I will invest in myself to know it so my children can know it. Parents we must give our children a head start in life and not hold them accountable for the mistakes in our own life.

Sit your child down and ask them what their plans are and not yours. If they want to stay with you and they have a job, you need to let them know right then that you expect them to pay bills and which ones, they should not be paying all your bills. Give the child a chance to save and if they have a plan then they will save but for the children that think that they will blow all their money, increase the bills after some time, but give them the benefit of doubt if they have a plan in place. One way to know if your child has a plan is to ask them questions like where do you want to live, what kind of car do you need right now etc. so they can learn to save for something, if not they will waste it on nothing. Parents we can do this, it takes a village to raise children, but you will have to go to the village to get help and that is why this book was important to me, so I can help parents and their children become successful.

20 things you must do to become Successful

1. You must put God First in everything you do.
2. You must have in your mind what you need to change and in order to be successful. A made-up mind.
3. You must prepare early in the mornings. Even when you're not feeling like it.
4. You must be a giver, expecting nothing in return.

5. You must care more than others.
6. You must be a leader even if no one follows yet.
7. You must work even when your body says no.
8. You must be a risk taker.
9. You must look like a fool when you are researching for answers and asking questions.
10. You must invest in yourself at All cost.
11. You must fail and then get up and try again.
12. You must keep moving even when you have no breathe left to continue.
13. You must be compassionate towards those that treat you wrong.
14. You must meet deadlines and stay on schedule.
15. You must be accountable for the wrong decisions in your life.
16. You must keep moving when life throws curved balls.
17. You must always Stay Focused.
18. You must make mistakes and look like an idiot.
19. You must make out time for yourself each day.
20. You must have faith in Yourself.

You must do the hard things and the things that no one else will do for yourself. Hard things are the things that people do not want to do because it challenges a person at all levels within themselves. Successful people do the hard things in life and the poor people do the easy things in life. That is how you can differentiate a person with poverty mindset from a person with a wealthy mindset. It is the determination in not giving up no matter what happens in life. Successful people cry then get up and do something about the situation. Poor people cry and become depressed because no one will give it to them. My question to you is How bad do you want to be Successful and live your Best life, how bad do you want IT. It All starts with You.

UNCOMFORTABLE SEASON

Have you ever been in a situation that you felt uncomfortable and you did not know what to do? We all had those seasons that everything under the sun is going wrong from mental, physical, emotion, spiritual and financial. That's when you feel so frustrated and unable to fix the problems in your life. When you find yourself in that situation, be aware that you are approaching a storm. In situations like that, one thing you need to do is to take a deep breath and get a plan. First get rid of the heaviness you are experiencing by either crying or yelling, just vent it out so that you can get started on a solution. When you are going into a storm you need to decide a plan right away. For instance, when the weather guy tells you that a storm is coming, you start preparing for the storm. If he says it's going to rain, you dress for the rain. you get an umbrella and leave earlier for work because of the rain. When he tells you, a snowstorm is coming you go get food, pay all bills that's needed because you know you cannot go outside. When you know a storm is coming start to preparing, when your boss tells you that if you miss one more day you will be terminated start looking for another job, filing out application everywhere, you don't wait until you are terminated before you start to look for another job. All you are doing is preparing for the storm before the storm hits. When you know that you cannot pay your rent and you are already 1 month behind already and the next month is approaching fast, you start looking for another place to live, you don't wait until the last minute. When you know that the storm is coming, you start your preparation. Remember the Serenity prayer "God grant me the serenity to accept the things I cannot change, the courage to change the things I can and the wisdom to know the difference. Living one day at a time enjoying one moment at a time accepting hardship as a pathway to peace hardship just as Jesus did in this sinful world. Somethings in life we do not have control over, and we can only handle the things that are in our control. The things that is out of our control is a test. We must endeavor to learn something from the storm that we are in and if we do not pass the test we will be tested again with another storm. We go through things in life so that we can become strong. Remember the old saying "what does not kill you will make you stronger". In the bible terms Philippians 4:13 I can do all things through Christ who strengthens me.

You will learn what you are capable of handling. I went through many storms in my life. I remember one storm that I had was with my business partner. I had a bad business partner that did some horrible things to me that I was so hurt and didn't think I was going to recover, because when someone messes with your money, a different side of you comes out. At several points, I felt like it was the worst season of my life. But I had to remind myself that I have been through tougher storms before. Yes, I couldn't sleep or concentrate. I had sleepless night, was worried, upset and all of that, because sometimes you must vent that anger and frustration out in order to keep up with life. But that experience taught me a valuable lesson with partnerships. Also, when God is getting ready to elevate you to another level you will be tested on your strength and faithfulness on what you allow God to handle. God will never put more on you than you can bear. If you are going through the storm, you have the tools to make it through the storm and learn whatever it is that God is trying to show you at the time. Your faith will always be tested. God wants to see if you will trust in him totally when there is no one else, God will test you to see if you are faithful when you get everything that you wanted. He will also test you when you do not have the things that you wanted. Whether you are Rich or Poor, we will all go through some type of storm either mentally, physically, emotionally or financially.

You can have money and be depressed all at the same time with all the pressure of the people that are around you. You could be rich and still be diagnosed with a sickness that medicine cannot heal. or you could be lonely not knowing who to trust around you, not even your family. Everyone is going through a storm. Storms come and go they never stop; you can come out of one thing and then there is another issue you are facing. It may not be as bad as the last storm, maybe just showers and not a thunderstorm but it's still a storm. When the disciples were on the boat and a storm hit them, Jesus was sleep and everyone was scared so they woke up Jesus and Jesus said "why are you afraid, you have little faith, then Jesus told the storm "Peace be still" and the storm stopped. You have to speak to your storm and let your storm know who you are. You are a healer in Jesus name, Jehovah Jira is my provider. I am the head and not the tail. Bank accounts you are filled with money to take care of my family. When your kids start acting out, speak to them "you are a great kid and the devil is a liar if he thinks he will destroy you". God said that we can have life and have it more abundantly, but the abundance will come with work. Proverbs 18:21 Death and life are in the power of the tongue, and those who love it will eat its fruit. When you are in a storm, watch what you say and how you respond to others. Sometimes we bring storms upon ourselves because of what we have said about someone else or done to someone. For instance if you talk ill about other people's kids, it may come back to your kids, You shouldn't be saying things like I'm broke, I can't afford that, or I wish I had their money, when you don't know what that person had to go through to get that money, house or car. You can repeatedly keep saying those things and God gives it to you or put you in that person's place that you talked about. Just learn to stay humble and quiet and pay attention when you are going through a storm, there's always something you must learn. Most times when you are going through a storm, God is trying to show you something and give you the direction through the storm but if you are worrying, angry, and frustrated you cannot focus on God's voice and he cannot lead you through the storm. When going through a storm, you must be very quiet, so you can hear clearly.

Storms usually come with a lot of noise called distractions, so that your eyes and ears are focused on the problem instead of the lesson. Like in the movie Bird Box, they had to cover up their eyes and only be led by their other senses. Learning to open your other senses can save your life; your spirit man will always guide you in the right direction. When you're in a storm stop fretting or telling people what you are going through. Everyone does not need to know you are going through something. Continuously talking about a problem keeps the problem around longer because you keep speaking it into existence. Talk to God about the problem and leave it at the altar. 1 Peter 5:7

Casting all your cares upon Him, for He cares for you. When you cast your cares and tell God about the situation and how you feel, then you walk away. It's not your business how God fixes the situation. God just want you to leave it with him. Leaving a situation with God means that you will not discuss it with anyone else because God is taken care of the situation. God already knows what you are going through, and he just wants you to come to him and talk to him about it, so you can have a relationship with him. Instead of complaining to other people that cannot save you. People are going through their own issues and need comfort too. Whatever storm that you are going through, someone else has already been through it before, but this is your own experience which you must overcome, so you can show and tell someone else that goes through the same storm how you went through and how to make it out.

EXERCISE

How is your health at the current moment?

Do you exercise or do you desire to enjoy a healthy lifestyle? You can gain all the success in the world and if your health is not good, you will not be able to enjoy the success that you have worked so hard to achieve in your life. You can find so many exercising apps on your phones from 7 minute to 30 minutes and up. You can walk for 30 minutes a day around your apartment complex or your neighborhood. Working out helps your brain to learn how to relax. It also helps you clear your mind of everything. Exercising helps with stress for day to day activities. If you don't exercise, your muscles will become flabby and weak. Your heart and lungs won't function efficiently. And your joints will be stiff and easily injured. Inactivity is as much of a health risk as smoking! People who work out at least 3 times a week live longer and worry less than people who do not work out. Exercise may block negative thoughts or distract you from daily worries. Exercising with others provides an opportunity for increased social contact. Increased fitness may lift your mood and improve your sleep patterns. Exercise may also change levels of chemicals in your brain, such as serotonin, endorphins and stress hormones. Doing any physical activity is better than doing none. If you currently do no physical activity, start by doing some, and gradually build up to the recommended amount. You can start by working on getting into your best shape. No one can work out for you. When you look good, you feel good and you can think good. But you must do the work. I have listed at the end of the book some weight products to help you lose weight and gain energy. You will find products for CBD detox tea, regular detox tea, vitamins, toothpaste, hair and skin growth and many other products. See back of book for details and let's transform your health, because your health is a part of your wealth. Your family needs you around when you practice good healthy habits your family will too. Let's start with a healthier you.

CONCLUSION

I hope that this book was a blessing to you and your future. Everything that I discussed in the book; I have lived it. I want to help as many women as possible to become the best person and mother that they can be. If I helped only one woman with the book, I have done my job that God set before me. If you know any other woman, family, friend, daughter, sister, auntie, mother, mother-in-law, anybody that can benefit from this book have them to purchase a copy and be blessed. I hope that I have given you clarity on some of the issues that a woman and a mother go through and know how to come out of the dark situations that we all face as women and mothers. When you know better you will do better. Hosea 4:6 My people are destroyed for lack of knowledge. Because you have rejected knowledge, I also will reject you from being priest for Me; Because you have forgotten the law of your God. I also will forget your children. When you do not know, you just do not know. But when God sends people in your life to teach you things, humble yourself and take hid to what they are saying to help you along your journey. This is not all about your life, it's about your children, children future. I hope this book has encouraged and motivated you to live a happy, healthy and prosperous life. Thank you for taking the time out to purchase and read my book. Every book has been blessed and anointed by God just for you.

RESOURCES

Website:
lashielaholmes.com

Weight loss products go to:
http://bit.ly/DatTea

Questions about the Weight Loss Program:
tea@lashielaholmes.com

Life Insurance: Email me at
info@lashielaholmes.com

Income Taxes/Accounting
hptaxes@yahoo.com

Social media sites-Please follow me at:
Periscope- @lashielaholmes
Facebook-@lashielaholmes
Instagram-@lashielaholmes

www.ingramcontent.com/pod-product-compliance
Lightning Source LLC
Chambersburg PA
CBHW022120090426
42743CB00008B/931